Marx
Joyce
Abbott
Hardy
Cooper
Emerson
Austen
Defoe
Montaigne
Machiavelli
Chesterton
Hugo
Melville
Haggard
Eliot
Grimm
Stoker
Carroll
Christie
Molière
Wilde
Maupassant
Byron
Schiller
Engels
Garnett
Fitzgerald
Hawthorne
Smith
Kafka
Goethe
Einstein
Dostoyevsky
Hall
Cotton
Kipling
Doyle
Willis
Baum
Henry
Nietzsche
Leslie
Dumas
Flaubert
Turgenev
Balzac
Stockton
Vatsyayana
Crane
Burroughs
Verne
Curtis
Tocqueville
Gogol
Vinci
Homer
Widger
Tolstoy
Whitman
Busch
Darwin
Thoreau
Twain
Scott
Potter
Freud
Zola
Lawrence
Plato
Harte
Kant
Jowett
Stevenson
Dickens
Burton
Hesse
Andersen
London
Descartes
Cervantes
Voltaire
Poe
Aristotle
Wells
Cooke
Hale
James
Hastings
Bunner
Shakespeare
Irving
Richter
Chambers
Doré
Dante
Chekhov
Benedict
Alcott
Swift
Shaw
Pushkin
Wodehouse
Newton

 tredition®

Memoirs of Louis XIV and His Court and of the Regency — Volume 15

Louis de Rouvroy, duc de Saint-Simon

Imprint

This book is part of TREDITION CLASSICS

Author: Louis de Rouvroy, duc de Saint-Simon
Cover design: Buchgut, Berlin – Germany

Publisher: tredition GmbH, Hamburg - Germany
ISBN: 978-3-8424-5362-3

www.tredition.com
www.tredition.de

Copyright:
The content of this book is sourced from the public domain.

The intention of the TREDITION CLASSICS series is to make world literature in the public domain available in printed format. Literary enthusiasts and organizations, such as Project Gutenberg, worldwide have scanned and digitally edited the original texts. tredition has subsequently formatted and redesigned the content into a modern reading layout. Therefore, we cannot guarantee the exact reproduction of the original format of a particular historic edition. Please also note that no modifications have been made to the spelling, therefore it may differ from the orthography used today.

MEMOIRS OF LOUIS XIV AND HIS COURT AND OF THE REGENCY

BY

THE DUKE OF SAINT-SIMON

VOLUME 15.

CHAPTER CXIII

Few events of importance had taken place during my absence in Spain. Shortly after my return, however, a circumstance occurred which may fairly claim description from me. Let me, therefore, at once relate it.

Cardinal Dubois, every day more and more firmly established in the favour of M. le Duc d'Orleans, pined for nothing less than to be declared prime minister. He was already virtually in that position, but was not publicly or officially recognised as being so. He wished, therefore, to be declared.

One great obstacle in his path was the Marechal de Villeroy, with whom he was on very bad terms, and whom he was afraid of transforming into an open and declared enemy, owing to the influence the Marechal exerted over others. Tormented with agitating thoughts, every day that delayed his nomination seemed to him a year. Dubois became doubly ill-tempered and capricious, more and more inaccessible, and accordingly the most pressing and most important business was utterly neglected. At last he resolved to make a last effort at reconciliation with the Marechal, but mistrusting his own powers, decided upon asking Cardinal Bissy to be the mediator between them.

Bissy with great willingness undertook the peaceful commission; spoke to Villeroy, who appeared quite ready to make friends with Dubois, and even consented to go and see him. As chance would have it, he went, accompanied by Bissy, on Tuesday morning. I at the same time went, as was my custom, to Versailles to speak to M. le Duc d'Orleans upon some subject, I forget now what.

It was the day on which the foreign ministers had their audience of Cardinal Dubois, and when Bissy and Villeroy arrived, they found these ministers waiting in the chamber adjoining the Cardinal's cabinet.

The established usage is that they have their audience according to the order in which they arrive, so as to avoid all disputes among them as to rank and precedence. Thus Bissy and Villeroy found Dubois closeted with the Russian minister. It was proposed to inform the Cardinal at once, of a this, so rare as a visit from the Marechal de Villeroy; but the Marechal would not permit it, and sat down upon a sofa with Bissy to wait like the rest.

The audience being over, Dubois came from his cabinet, conducting the Russian minister, and immediately saw his sofa so well ornamented. He saw nothing but that in fact; on the instant he ran there, paid a thousand compliments to the Marechal for anticipating him, when he was only waiting for permission to call upon him, and begged him and Bissy to step into the cabinet. While they were going there, Dubois made his excuses to the ambassadors for attending to Villeroy before them, saying that his functions and his assiduity as governor of the King did not permit him to be long absent from the presence of his Majesty; and with this compliment he quitted them and returned into his cabinet.

At first nothing passed but reciprocal compliments and observations from Cardinal Bissy, appropriate to the subject. Then followed protestations from Dubois and replies from the Marechal. Thus far, the sea was very smooth. But absorbed in his song, the Marechal began to forget its tune; then to plume himself upon his frankness and upon his plain speaking; then by degrees, growing hot in his honours, he gave utterance to divers naked truths, closely akin to insults.

Dubois, much astonished, pretended not to feel the force of these observations, but as they increased every moment, Bissy tried to call back the Marechal, explain things to him, and give a more pleasant tone to the conversation. But the mental tide had begun to rise, and now it was entirely carrying away the brains of Villeroy. From bad to worse was easy. The Marechal began now to utter unmistakable insults and the most bitter reproaches. In vain Bissy tried to silence him; representing to him how far he was wandering from the subject they came to talk upon; how indecent it was to insult a man in his own house, especially, after arriving on purpose to conclude a reconciliation with him. All Bissy could say simply had the effect of exasperating the Marechal, and of making him vomit forth the most extravagant insults that insolence and disdain could suggest.

Dubois, stupefied and beside himself, was deprived of his tongue, could not utter a word; while Bissy, justly inflamed with anger, uselessly tried to interrupt his friend. In the midst of the sudden fire which had seized the Marechal, he had placed himself in such a manner that he barred the passage to the door, and he continued his invectives without restraint. Tired of insults, he passed to menaces and derision, saying to Dubois that since he had now thrown off all disguise, they no longer were on terms to pardon each other, and then he assured Dubois that, sooner or later, he would do him all the injury possible, and gave him what he called good counsel.

"You are all powerful," said he; "everybody bends before you; nobody resists you; what are the greatest people in the land compared with you? Believe me, you have only one thing to do; employ all your power, put yourself at ease, and arrest me, if you dare. Who can hinder you? Arrest me, I say, you have only that course open."

Thereupon, he redoubled his challenges and his insults, like a man who is thoroughly persuaded that between arresting him and scaling Heaven there is no difference. As may well be imagined, such astounding remarks were not uttered without interruption, and warm altercations from the Cardinal de Bissy, who, nevertheless, could not stop the torrent. At last, carried away by anger and vexation, Bissy seized the Marechal by the arm and the shoulder, and hurried him to the door, which he opened, and then pushed him out, and followed at his heels. Dubois, more dead than alive, followed also, as well as he could—he was obliged to be on his guard against the foreign ministers who were waiting. But the three disputants vainly tried to appear composed; there was not one of the ministers who did not perceive that some violent scene must have passed in the cabinet, and forthwith Versailles was filled with this news; which was soon explained by the bragging, the explanations, the challenges, and the derisive speeches of the Marechal de Villeroy.

I had worked and chatted for a long time with M. le Duc d'Orleans. He had passed into his wardrobe, and I was standing behind his bureau arranging his papers when I saw Cardinal Dubois enter like a whirlwind, his eyes starting out of his head. Seeing me alone, he screamed rather than asked, "Where is M. le Duc d'Orleans?" I replied that he had gone into his wardrobe, and seeing him so overturned, I asked him what was the matter.

"I am lost, I am lost!" he replied, running to the wardrobe. His reply was so loud and so sharp that M. le Duc d'Orleans, who heard it, also ran forward, so that they met each other in the doorway. They returned towards me, and the Regent asked what was the matter.

Dubois, who always stammered, could scarcely speak, so great was his rage and fear; but he succeeded at last in acquainting us with the details I have just given, although at greater length. He concluded by saying that after the insults he had received so treacherously, and in a manner so basely premeditated, the Regent must choose between him and the Marechal de Villeroy, for that after what had passed he could not transact any business or remain at the Court in safety and honour, while the Marechal de Villeroy remained there!

I cannot express the astonishment into which M. le Duc d'Orleans and I were thrown. We could not believe what we had heard, but fancied we were dreaming. M. le Duc d'Orleans put several questions to Dubois, I took the liberty to do the same, in order to sift the affair to the bottom. But there was no variation in the replies of the Cardinal, furious as he was. Every moment he presented the same option to the Regent; every moment he proposed that the Cardinal de Bissy should be sent for as having witnessed everything. It may be imagined that this second scene, which I would gladly have escaped, was tolerably exciting.

The Cardinal still insisting that the Regent must choose which of the two be sent away, M. le Duc d'Orleans asked me what I thought. I replied that I was so bewildered and so moved by this astounding occurrence that I must collect myself before speaking. The Cardinal, without addressing himself to me but to M. le Duc d'Orleans, who he saw was plunged Memoirs in embarrassment, strongly insisted that he must come to some resolution. Upon this M. le Duc d'Orleans beckoned me over, and I said to him that hitherto I had always regarded the dismissal of the Marechal de Villeroy as a very dangerous enterprise, for reasons I had several times alleged to his Royal Highness: but that now whatever peril there might be in undertaking it, the frightful scene that had just been enacted persuaded me that it would be much more dangerous to leave him near the King than to get rid of him altogether. I added that this was my opinion, since his Royal Highness wished to know it without giving me the time to reflect upon it with more coolness; but as for the execution, that must be well discussed before being attempted.

Whilst I spoke, the Cardinal pricked up his ears, turned his eyes upon me, sucked in all my words, and changed colour like a man who hears his doom pronounced. My opinion relieved him as much as the rage with which he was filled permitted. M. le Duc d'Orleans approved what I had just said, and the Cardinal, casting a glance upon me as of thanks, said he was the master, and must choose, but that he must choose at once, because things could not remain as they were. Finally, it was agreed that the rest of the day (it was now about twelve) and the following morning should be given to reflection upon the matter, and that the next day, at three o'clock in the afternoon, I should meet M. le Duc d'Orleans.

The next day accordingly I went to M. le Prince, whom I found with the Cardinal Dubois. M. le Duc entered a moment after, quite full of the adventure. Cardinal Dubois did not fail, though, to give him an abridged recital of it, loaded with comments and reflections. He was more his own master than on the preceding day, having had time to recover himself, we cherishing hopes that the Marechal would be sent to the right about. It was here that I heard of the brag of the Marechal de Villeroy concerning the struggle he had had with Dubois, and of the challenges and insults he had uttered with a confidence which rendered his arrest more and more necessary.

After we had chatted awhile, standing, Dubois went away. M. le Duc d'Orleans sat down at his bureau, and M. le Duc and I sat in front of him. There we deliberated upon what ought to be done. After a few words of explanation from the Regent, he called upon me to give my opinion. I did so as briefly as possible, repeating what I had said on the previous day. M. le Duc d'Orleans, during my short speech, was very attentive, but with the countenance of a man much embarrassed.

As soon as I had finished, he asked M. le Duc what he thought. M. le Duc said his opinion was mine, and that if the Marechal de Villeroy remained in his office there was nothing for it but to put the key outside the door; that was his expression. He reproduced some of the principal reasons I had alleged, supported them, and concluded by saying there was not a moment to lose. M. le Duc d'Orleans summed up a part of what had been said, and agreed that the Marechal de Villeroy must be got rid of. M. le Duc again remarked that it must be done at once. Then we set about thinking how we could do it.

M. le Duc d'Orleans asked me my advice thereon. I said there were two things to discuss, the pretext and the execution. That a pretext was necessary, such as would convince the impartial, and be unopposed even by the friends of the Marechal de Villeroy; that above all things we had to take care to give no one ground for believing that the disgrace of Villeroy was the fruit of the insults he had heaped upon Cardinal Dubois; that outrageous as those insults might be, addressed to a cardinal, to a minister in possession of entire confidence, and at the head of affairs, the public, who envied him and did not like him, well remembering whence he had sprung, would consider the victim too illustrious; that the chastisement would overbalance the offence, and would be complained of; that violent resolutions, although necessary, should always have reason and appearances in their favour; that therefore I was against allowing punishment to follow too quickly upon the real offence, inasmuch as M. le Duc d'Orleans had one of the best pretexts in the world for disgracing the Marechal, a pretext known by everybody, and which would be admitted by everybody.

I begged the Regent then to remember that he had told me several times he never had been able to speak to the King in private, or even in a whisper before others; that when he had tried, the Marechal de Villeroy had at once come forward poking his nose between them, and declaring that while he was governor he would never suffer any one, not even his Royal Highness, to address his Majesty in a low tone, much lest to speak to him in private. I said that this conduct towards the Regent, a grandson of France, and the nearest relative the King had, was insolence enough to disgust every one, and apparent as such at half a glance. I counselled M. le Duc d'Orleans to make use of this circumstance, and by its means to lay a trap for the Marechal into which there was not the slightest doubt he would fall. The trap was to be thus arranged. M. le Duc d'Orleans was to insist upon his right to speak to the King in private, and upon the refusal of the Marechal to recognise it, was to adopt a new tone and make Villeroy feel he was the master. I added, in conclusion, that this snare must not be laid until everything was ready to secure its success.

When I had ceased speaking, "You have robbed me," said the Regent; "I was going to propose the same thing if you had not. What do you think of it, Monsieur?" regarding M. le Duc. That Prince strongly approved the proposition I had just made, briefly praised every part of it, and added that he saw nothing better to be done than to execute this plan very punctually.

It was agreed afterwards that no other plan could be adopted than that of arresting the Marechal and sending him right off at once to Villeroy, and then, after having allowed him to repose there a day or two, on account of his age, but well watched, to see if he should be sent on to Lyons or elsewhere. The manner in which he was to be arrested was to be decided at Cardinal Dubois' apartments, where the Regent begged me to go at once. I rose accordingly, and went there.

I found Dubois with one or two friends, all of whom were in the secret of this affair, as he, at once told me, to put me at my ease. We soon therefore entered upon business, but it would be superfluous to relate here all that passed in this little assembly. What we resolved on was very well executed, as will be seen. I arranged with Le Blanc, who was one of the conclave, that the instant the arrest had taken place, he should send to Meudon, and simply inquire after me; nothing more, and that by this apparently meaningless compliment, I should know that the Marechal had been packed off.

I returned towards evening to Meudon, where several friends of Madame de Saint-Simon and of myself often slept, and where others, following the fashion established at Versailles and Paris, came to dine or sup, so that the company was always very numerous. The scene between Dubois and Villeroy was much talked about, and the latter universally blamed. Neither then nor during the ten days which elapsed before his arrest, did it enter into the head of anybody to suppose that anything worse would happen to him than general blame for his unmeasured violence, so accustomed were people to his freaks, and to the feebleness of M. le Duc d'Orleans. I was now delighted, however, to find such general confidence, which augmented that of the Marechal, and rendered more easy the execution of our project against him; punishment he more and more deserved by the indecency and affectation of his discourses, and the audacity of his continual challenges.

Three or four days after, I went to Versailles, to see M. le Duc d'Orleans. He said that, for want of a better, and in consequence of what I had said to him on more than one occasion of the Duc de Charost, it was to him he intended to give the office of governor of the King: that he had secretly seen him that Charost had accepted with willingness the post, and was now safely shut up in his apartment at Versailles, seeing no one, and seen by no one, ready to be led to the King the moment the time should arrive. The Regent went over with me all the measures to be taken, and I returned to Meudon, resolved not to budge from it until they were executed, there being nothing more to arrange.

On Sunday, the 12th of August, 1722, M. le Duc d'Orleans went, towards the end of the afternoon, to work with the King, as he was accustomed to do several times each week; and as it was summer time now, he went after his airing, which he always took early. This work was to show the King by whom were to be filled up vacant places in the church, among the magistrates and intendants, &c., and to briefly explain to him the reasons which suggested the selection, and sometimes the distribution of the finances. The Regent informed him, too, of the foreign news, which was within his comprehension, before it was made public. At the conclusion of this labour, at which the Marechal de Villeroy was always present, and sometimes M. de Frejus (when he made bold to stop), M. le Duc d'Orleans begged the King to step into a little back cabinet, where he would say a word to him alone.

The Marechal de Villeroy at once opposed. M. le Duc d'Orleans, who had laid this snare far him, saw him fall into it with satisfaction. He represented to the Marechal that the King was approaching the age when he would govern by himself, that it was time for him, who was meanwhile the depository of all his authority, to inform him of things which he could understand, and which could only be explained to him alone, whatever confidence might merit any third person. The Regent concluded by begging the Marechal to cease to place any obstacles in the way of a thing so necessary and so important, saying that he had, perhaps, to reproach himself for,—solely out of complaisance to him, not having coerced before.

The Marechal, arising and stroking his wig, replied that he knew the respect he owed, him, and knew also quite as well the respect he owed to the King, and to his place, charged as he was with the person of his Majesty, and being responsible for it. But he said he would not suffer his Royal Highness to speak to the King in private (because he ought to know everything said to his Majesty), still less would he suffer him to lead the King into a cabinet, out of his sight, for 'twas his (the Marechal's) duty never to lose sight of his charge, and in everything to answer for it.

Upon this, M. le Duc d'Orleans looked fixedly at the Marechal and said, in the tone of a master, that he mistook himself and forgot himself; that he ought to remember to whom he was speaking, and take care what words he used; that the respect he (the Regent) owed to the presence of the King, hindered him from replying as he ought to reply, and from continuing this conversation. Therefore he made a profound reverence to the King, and went away.

The Marechal, thoroughly angry, conducted him some steps, mumbling and gesticulating; M. le Duc d'Orleans pretending to neither see nor hear him, the King astonished, and M. de Frejus laughing in his sleeve. The bait so well swallowed,—no one doubted that the Marechal, audacious as he was, but nevertheless a servile and timid courtier, would feel all the difference between braving, bearding, and insulting Cardinal Dubois (odious to everybody, and always smelling of the vile egg from which he had been hatched) and wrestling with the Regent in the presence of the King, claiming to annihilate M. le Duc d'Orleans' rights and authority, by appealing to his own pretended rights and authority as governor of the King. People were not mistaken; less than two hours after what had occurred, it was known that the Marechal, bragging of what he had just done, had added that he should consider himself very unhappy if M. le Duc d'Orleans thought he had been wanting in respect to him, when his only idea was to fulfil his precious duty; and that he would go the next day to have an explanation with his Royal Highness, which he doubted not would be satisfactory to him.

At every hazard, all necessary measures had been taken as soon as the day was fixed on which the snare was to be laid for the Marechal. Nothing remained but to give form to them directly it was known that on the morrow the Marechal would come and throw himself into the lion's mouth.

Beyond the bed-room of M. le Duc d'Orleans was a large and fine cabinet, with four big windows looking upon the garden, and on the same floor, two paces distant, two other windows; and two at the side in front of the chimney, and all these windows opened like doors. This cabinet occupied the corner where the courtiers awaited, and behind was an adjoining cabinet, where M. le Duc d'Orleans worked and received distinguished persons or favourites who wished to talk with him.

The word was given. Artagnan, captain of the grey musketeers, was in the room (knowing what was going to happen), with many trusty officers of his company whom he had sent for, and former musketeers to be made use of at a pinch, and who clearly saw by these preparations that something important was in the wind, but without divining what. There were also some light horse posted outside these windows in the same ignorance, and many principal officers and others in the Regent's bed-room, and in the grand cabinet.

All things being well arranged, the Marechal de Villeroy arrived about mid-day, with his accustomed hubbub, but alone, his chair and porters remaining outside, beyond the Salle des Gardes. He enters like a comedian, stops, looks round, advances some steps. Under pretext of civility, he is environed, surrounded. He asks in an authoritative tone, what M. le Duc d'Orleans is doing: the reply is, he is in his private room within.

The Marechal elevates his tone, says that nevertheless he must see the Regent; that he is going to enter; when lo! La Fare, captain of M. le Duc d'Orleans' guards, presents himself before him, arrests him, and demands his sword. The Marechal becomes furious, all present are in commotion. At this instant Le Blanc presents himself. His sedan chair, that had been hidden, is planted before the Marechal. He cries aloud, he is shaking on his lower limbs; but he is thrust into the chair, which is closed upon him and carried away in the twinkling of an eye through one of the side windows into the garden, La Fare and Artagnan each on one side of the chair, the light horse and musketeers behind, judging only by the result what was in the wind. The march is hastened; the party descend the steps of the orangery by the side of the thicket; the grand gate is found open and a coach and six before it. The chair is put down; the Marechal storms as he will; he is cast into the coach; Artagnan mounts by his side; an officer of the musketeers is in front; and one of the gentlemen in ordinary of the King by the side of the officer; twenty musketeers, with mounted officers, surround the vehicle, and away they go.

This side of the garden is beneath the window of the Queen's apartments (when occupied by the Infanta). This scene under the blazing noon-day sun was seen by no one, and although the large number of persons in M. le Duc d'Orleans' rooms soon dispersed, it is astonishing that an affair of this kind remained unknown more than ten hours in the chateau of Versailles. The servants of the Marechal de Villeroy (to whom nobody had dared to say a word) still waited with their master's chair near the Salle des Gardes. They were, told, after M. le Duc d'Orleans had seen the King, that the Marechal had gone to Villeroy, and that they could carry to him what was necessary.

I received at Meudon the message arranged. I was sitting down to table, and it was only towards the supper that people came from Versailles to tell us all the news, which was making much sensation there, but a sensation very measured on account of the surprise and fear paused by the manner in which the arrest had been executed.

It was no agreeable task, that which had to be performed soon after by the Regent; I mean when he carried the news of the arrest to the King. He entered into his Majesty's cabinet, which he cleared of all the company it contained, except those people whose post gave them aright to enter, but of them there were not many present. At the first word, the King reddened; his eyes moistened; he hid his face against the back of an armchair, without saying a word; would neither go out nor play. He ate but a few mouthfuls at supper, wept, and did not sleep all night. The morning and the dinner of the next day, the 14th, passed off but little better.

CHAPTER CXIV

That same 14th, as I rose from dinner at Meudon, with much company, the valet de chambre who served me said that a courier from Cardinal Dubois had a letter for me, which he had not thought good to bring me before all my guests. I opened the letter. The Cardinal conjured me to go instantly and see him at Versailles, bringing with me a trusty servant, ready to be despatched to La Trappe, as soon as I had spoken with him, and not to rack my brains to divine what this might mean, because it would be impossible to divine it, and that he was waiting with the utmost impatience to tell it to me. I at once ordered my coach, which I thought a long time in coming from the stables. They are a considerable distance from the new chateau I occupied.

This courier to be taken to the Cardinal, in order to be despatched to La Trappe, turned my head. I could not imagine what had happened to occupy the Cardinal so thoroughly so soon after the arrest of Villeroy. The constitution, or some important and unknown fugitive discovered at La Trappe, and a thousand other thoughts, agitated me until I arrived at Versailles.

Upon reaching the chateau, I saw Dubois at a window awaiting me, and making many signs to me, and upon reaching the staircase, I found him there at the bottom, as I was about to mount. His first word was to ask me if I had brought with me a man who could post to La Trappe. I showed him my valet de chambre, who knew the road well, having travelled over it with me very often, and who was well known to the Cardinal, who, when simple Abbe Dubois, used very frequently to chat with him while waiting for me.

The Cardinal explained to me, as we ascended the stairs, the cause of his message. Immediately after the departure of the Marechal de Villeroy, M. le Frejus, the King's instructor, had been missed. He had disappeared. He had not slept at Versailles. No one knew what had become of him! The grief of the King had so much increased upon receiving this fresh blow—both his familiar friends taken from him at once—that no one knew what to do with him. He was in the most violent despair, wept bitterly, and could not be pacified. The Cardinal concluded by saying that no stone must be left unturned in order to find M. de Frejus. That unless he had gone to Villeroy, it was probable he had hid himself in La Trappe, and that we must send and see. With this he led me to M. le Duc d'Orleans. He was alone, much troubled, walking up and down his chamber, and he said to me that he knew not what would become of the King, or what to do with him; that he was crying for M. de Frejus, and—would listen to nothing; and the Regent began himself to cry out against this strange flight.

After some further consideration, Dubois pressed me to go and write to La Trappe. All was in disorder where we were; everybody spoke at once in the cabinet; it was impossible, in the midst of all this noise, to write upon the bureau, as I often did when I was alone with the King. My apartment was in the new wing, and perhaps shut up, for I was not expected that day. I went therefore, instead, into the chamber of Peze, close at hand, and wrote my letter there. The letter finished, and I about to descend, Peze, who had left me, returned, crying, "He is found! he is found! your letter is useless; return to M. le Duc d'Orleans."

He then related to me that just before, one of M. le Duc d'Orleans' people, who knew that Frejus was a friend of the Lamoignons, had met Courson in the grand court, and had asked him if he knew what had become of Frejus; that Courson had replied, "Certainly: he went last night to sleep at Basville, where the President Lamoignon is;" and that upon this, the man hurried Courson to M. le Duc d'Orleans to relate this to him.

Peze and I arrived at M. le Duc d'Orleans' room just after Courson left it. Serenity had returned. Frejus was well belaboured. After a moment of cheerfulness, Cardinal Dubois advised M. le Duc d'Orleans to go and carry this good news to the King, and to say that a courier should at once be despatched to Basville, to make his preceptor return. M. le Duc d'Orleans acted upon the suggestion, saying he would return directly. I remained with Dubois awaiting him.

After having discussed a little this mysterious flight of Frejus, Dubois told me he had news of Villeroy. He said that the Marechal had not ceased to cry out against the outrage committed upon his person, the audacity of the Regent, the insolence of Dubois, or to hector Artagnan all the way for having lent himself to such criminal violence; then he invoked the Manes of the deceased King, bragged of his confidence in him, the importance of the place he held, and for which he had been preferred above all others; talked of the rising that so impudent an enterprise would cause in Paris, throughout the realm, and in foreign countries; deplored the fate of the young King and of all the kingdom; the officers selected by the late King for the most precious of charges, driven away, the Duc du Maine first, himself afterwards; then he burst out into exclamations and invectives; then into praises of his services, of his fidelity, of his firmness, of his inviolable attachment to his duty. In fact, he was so astonished, so troubled, so full of vexation and of rage, that he was thoroughly beside himself. The Duc de Villeroy, the Marechal de Tallard and Biron had permission to go and see him at Villeroy: scarcely anybody else asked for it.

M. le Duc d'Orleans having returned from the King, saying that the news he had carried had much appeased his Majesty, we agreed we must so arrange matters that Frejus should return the next morning, that M. le Duc d'Orleans should receive him well, as though nothing had happened, and give him to understand that it was simply to avoid embarrassing him, that he had not been made aware of the secret of the arrest (explaining this to him with all the more liberty, because Frejus hated the Marechal, his haughtiness, his jealousy, his capriciousness, and in his heart must be delighted at his removal, and at being able to have entire possession of the—King), then beg him to explain to the King the necessity of Villeroy's dismissal: then communicate to Frejus the selection of the Duc de

Charost as governor of the King; promise him all the concert and the attention from this latter he could desire; ask him to counsel and guide Charost; finally, seize the moment of the King's joy at the return of Frejus to inform his Majesty of the new governor chosen, and to present Charost to him. All this was arranged and very well, executed next day.

When the Marechal heard of it at Villeroy, he flew into a strange passion against Charost (of whom he spoke with the utmost contempt for having accepted his place), but above all against Frejus, whom he called a traitor and a villain! His first moments of passion, of fury, and of transport, were all the more violent, because he saw by the tranquillity reigning everywhere that his pride had deceived him in inducing him to believe that the Parliament, the markets, all Paris would rise if the Regent dared to touch a person so important and so well beloved as he imagined himself to be. This truth, which he could no longer hide from himself, and which succeeded so rapidly to the chimeras that had been his food and his life, threw him into despair, and turned his head. He fell foul of the Regent, of his minister, of those employed to arrest him, of those who had failed to defend him, of all who had not risen in revolt to bring him back in triumph, of Charost, who had dared to succeed him, and especially of Frejus, who had deceived him in such an unworthy manner. Frejus was the person against whom he was the most irritated. Reproaches of ingratitude and of treachery rained unceasingly upon him; all that the Marechal had done for him with the deceased King was recollected; how he had protected, aided, lodged, and fed him; how without him (Villeroy) he (Frejus) would never have been preceptor of the King; and all this was exactly true.

The treachery to which he alluded he afterwards explained. He said that he and Frejus had agreed at the very commencement of the regency to act in union; and that if by troubles or events impossible to foresee, but which were only too common in regencies, one of them should be dismissed from office, the other not being able to hinder the dismissal, though not touched himself, should at once withdraw and never return to his post, until the first was reinstated in his. And after these explanations, new cries broke out against the perfidy of this miserable wretch—(for the most odious terms ran glibly from the end of his tongue)—who thought like a fool to cover his perfidy with a veil of gauze, in slipping off to Basville, so as to be instantly sought and brought back, in fear lest he should lose his place by the slightest resistance or the slightest delay, and who expected to acquit himself thus of his word, and of the reciprocal engagement both had taken; and then he returned to fresh insults and fury against this serpent, as he said, whom he had warmed and nourished so many years in his bosom.

The account of these transports and insults, promptly came from Villeroy to Versailles, brought, not only by the people whom the Regent had placed as guards over the Marechal, and to give an exact account of all he said and did, day by day, but by all the domestics who came and went, and before whom Villeroy launched out his speeches, at table, while passing through his ante-chambers, or while taking a turn in his gardens.

All this weighed heavily upon Frejus by the rebound. Despite the apparent tranquillity of his visage, he appeared confounded. He replied by a silence of respect and commiseration in which he enveloped himself; nevertheless, he could not do so to the Duc de Villeroy, the Marechal de Tallard, and a few others. He tranquilly said to them, that he had done all he could to fulfil an engagement which he did not deny, but that after having thus satisfied the call of honour, he did not think he could refuse to obey orders so express from the King and the Regent, or abandon the former in order to bring about the return of the Marechal de Villeroy, which was the object of their reciprocal engagement, and which he was certain he could not effect by absence, however prolonged. But amidst these very sober excuses could be seen the joy which peeped forth from him, in spite of himself, at being freed from so inconvenient a superior, at having to do with a new governor whom he could easily manage, at being able when he chose to guide himself in all liberty towards the grand object he had always desired, which was to attach himself to the King without reserve, and to make out of this attachment, obtained by all sorts of means, the means of a greatness which he did not yet dare to figure to himself, but which time and opportunity would teach him how to avail himself of in the best manner, marching to it meanwhile in perfect security.

The Marechal was allowed to refresh himself, and exhale his anger five or six days at Villeroy; and as he was not dangerous away from the King, he was sent to Lyons, with liberty to exercise his functions of governor of the town and province, measures being taken to keep a watch upon him, and Des Libois being left with him to diminish his authority by this manifestation of precaution and surveillance, which took from him all appearance of credit. He would receive no honours on arriving there. A large quantity of his first fire was extinguished; this wide separation from Paris and the Court, where not even the slightest movement had taken place, everybody being stupefied and in terror at an arrest of this importance; took from him all remaining hope, curbed his impetuosity, and finally induced him to conduct himself with sagacity in order to avoid worse treatment.

Such was the catastrophe of a man, so incapable of all the posts he had occupied, who displayed chimeras and audacity in the place of prudence and sagacity, who everywhere appeared a trifler and a comedian, and whose universal and profound ignorance (except of the meanest arts of the courtier) made plainly visible the thin covering of probity and of virtue with which he tried to hide his ingratitude, his mad ambition, his desire to overturn all in order to make himself the chief of all, in the midst of his weakness and his fears, and to hold a helm he was radically incapable of managing. I speak here only of his conduct since the establishment of the regency. Elsewhere, in more than one place, the little or nothing he was worth has been shown; how his ignorance and his jealousy lost us Flanders, and nearly ruined the State; how his felicity was pushed to the extreme, and what deplorable reverses followed his return. Sufficient to say that he never recovered from the state into which this last madness threw him, and that the rest of his life was only bitterness, regret, contempt! He had persuaded the King that it was he, alone, who by vigilance and precaution had preserved his life from poison that others wished to administer to him. This was the source of those tears shed by the King when Villeroy was carried off, and of his despair when Frejus disappeared. He did not doubt that both had been removed in order that this crime might be more easily committed.

The prompt return of Frejus dissipated the half, of his fear, the continuance of his good health delivered him by degrees from the other. The preceptor, who had a great interest in preserving the King, and who felt much relieved by the absence of Villeroy, left nothing undone in order to extinguish these gloomy ideas; and consequently to let blame fall upon him who had inspired them. He feared the return of the Marechal when the King, who was approaching his majority, should be the master; once delivered of the yoke he did not wish it to be reimposed upon him. He well knew that the grand airs, the ironies, the authoritative fussiness in public of the Marechal were insupportable to his Majesty, and that they held together only by those frightful ideas of poison. To destroy them was to show the Marechal uncovered, and worse than that to show to the King, without appearing to make a charge against the Marechal, the criminal interest he had in exciting these alarms, and the falsehood and atrocity of such a venomous invention. These reflections; which the health of the King each day confirmed, sapped all esteem, all gratitude, and left his Majesty in full liberty of conscience to prohibit, when he should be the master, all approach to his person on the part of so vile and so interested an impostor.

Frejus made use of these means to shelter himself against the possibility of the Marechal's return, and to attach himself to the King without reserve. The prodigious success of his schemes has been only too well felt since.

The banishment of Villeroy, flight and return of Frejus, and installation of Charost as governor of the King, were followed by the confirmation of his Majesty by the Cardinal de Rohan, and by his first communion, administered to him by this self-same Cardinal, his grand almoner.

CHAPTER CXV

Villeroy being banished, the last remaining obstacle in Dubois' path was removed. There was nothing: now, to hinder him from being proclaimed prime minister. I had opposed it as stoutly as I could; but my words were lost upon M. le Duc d'Orleans. Accordingly, about two o'clock in the afternoon of the 23rd of August, 1722, Dubois was declared prime minister by the Regent, and by the Regent at once conducted to the King as such.

After this event I began insensibly to withdraw from public affairs. Before the end of the year the King was consecrated at Rheims. The disorder at the ceremony was inexpressible. All precedent was forgotten. Rank was hustled and jostled, so to speak, by the crowd. The desire to exclude the nobility from all office and all dignity was obvious, at half a glance. My spirit was ulcerated at this; I saw approaching the complete re-establishment of the bastards; my heart was cleft in twain, to see the Regent at the heels of his unworthy minister. He was a prey to the interest, the avarice, the folly, of this miserable wretch, and no remedy possible. Whatever experience I might have had of the astonishing weakness of M. le Duc d'Orleans, it had passed all bounds when I saw him with my own eyes make Dubois prime minister, after all I had said to him on the subject,— after all he had said to me. The year 1723 commenced, and found me in this spirit. It is at the end of this year I have determined to end those memoirs, and the details of it will not be so full or so abundant as of preceding years. I was hopelessly wearied with M. le Duc d'Orleans; I no longer approached this poor prince (with so many great and useless talents buried in him)—except with repugnance. I could not help feeling for him what the poor, Israelites said to themselves in the desert about the manna: "Nauseat anima mea suffer cibum istum tevissimum." I no longer deigned to speak to him. He perceived this: I felt he was pained at it; he strove to reconcile me to him, without daring, however, to speak of affairs, except briefly, and with constraint, and yet he could not hinder himself from speaking of them. I scarcely took the trouble to reply to him, and I cut his conversation as short as possible. I abridged and curtailed my audiences with him; I listened to his reproaches with coldness. In fact, what had I to discuss with a Regent who was no longer one, not even over himself, still less over a realm plunged in disorder?

Cardinal Dubois, when he met me, almost courted me. He knew not how to catch me. The bonds which united me to M. le Duc d'Orleans had always been so strong that the prime minister, who knew their strength, did not dare to flatter himself he could break them. His resource was to try to disgust me by inducing his master to treat me with a reserve which was completely new to him, and which cost him more than it cost me; for, in fact, he had often found my confidence very useful to him, and had grown accustomed to it. As for me, I dispensed with his friendship more than willingly, vexed at being no longer able to gather any fruit from it for the advantage of the State or himself, wholly abandoned as he was to his Paris pleasures and to his minister. The conviction of my complete inutility more and more kept me in the background, without the slightest suspicion that different conduct could be dangerous to me, or that, weak and abandoned to Dubois as was the Regent, the former could ever exile me, like the Duc de Roailles, and Cariillac, or disgust me into exiling myself. I followed, then, my accustomed life. That is to say, never saw M. le Duc d'Orleans except tete-a-tete, and then very seldom at intervals that each time grew longer, coldly, briefly, never talking to him of business, or, if he did to me, returning the conversation, and replying it! a manner to make it drop. Acting thus, it is easy to see that I was mixed up in nothing, and what I shall have to relate now will have less of the singularity and instructiveness of good and faithful memoirs, than of the dryness and sterility of the gazettes.

First of all I will finish my account of Cardinal Dubois. I have very little more to say of him; for he had scarcely begun to enjoy his high honours when Death came to laugh at him for the sweating labour he had taken to acquire them.

On the 11th of June, 1723, the King went to reside at Meudon, ostensibly in order that the chateau of Versailles might be cleared — in reality, to accommodate Cardinal Dubois. He had just presided over the assembly of the day, and flattered to the last degree at this, wished to repose upon the honour. He desired, also, to be present sometimes at the assembling of the Company of the Indies. Meudon brought him half-way to Paris, and saved him a journey. His debauchery had so shattered his health that the movement of a coach gave him pains which he very carefully hid.

The King held at Meudon a review of his household, which in his pride the Cardinal must needs attend. It cost him dear. He mounted on horseback the better, to enjoy his triumph; he suffered cruelly, and became so violently ill that he was obliged to have assistance. The most celebrated doctors and physicians were called in, with great secrecy. They shook their heads, and came so often that news of the illness began to transpire. Dubois was unable to go to Paris again more than once or twice, and then with much trouble, and solely to conceal his malady, which gave him no repose.

He left nothing undone, in fact, to hide it from the world; he went as often as he could to the council; apprised the ambassadors he would go to Paris, and did not go; kept himself invisible at home, and bestowed the most frightful abuse upon everybody who dared to intrude upon him. On Saturday, the 7th of August, he was so ill that the doctors declared he must submit to an operation, which was very urgent, and without which he could hope to live but a few days; because the abscess he had having burst the day he mounted on horseback, gangrene had commenced, with an overflow of pus, and he must be transported, they added, to Versailles, in order to undergo this operation. The trouble this terrible announcement caused him, so overthrew him that he could not be moved the next day, Sunday, the 8th; but on Monday he was transported in a litter, at five o'clock in the morning.

After having allowed him to repose himself a, little, the doctors and surgeons proposed that he should receive the sacrament, and submit to the operation immediately after. This was not heard very peacefully; he had scarcely ever been free from fury since the day of the review; he had grown worse on Saturday, when the operation was first announced to him. Nevertheless, some little time after, he sent for a priest from Versailles, with whom he remained alone about a quarter of an hour. Such a great and good man, so well prepared for death, did not need more: Prime ministers, too, have privileged confessions. As his chamber again filled, it was proposed that he should take the viaticum; he cried out that that was soon said, but there was a ceremonial for the cardinals, of which he was ignorant, and Cardinal Bissy must be sent to, at Paris, for information upon it. Everybody looked at his neighbour, and felt that Dubois merely wished to gain time; but as the operation was urgent, they proposed it to him without further delay. He furiously sent them away, and would no longer hear talk of it.

The faculty, who saw the imminent danger of the slightest delay, sent to Meudon for M. le Duc d'Orleans, who instantly came in the first conveyance he could lay his hands on. He exhorted the Cardinal to suffer the operation; then asked the faculty, if it could be performed in safety. They replied that they could say nothing for certain, but that assuredly the Cardinal had not two hours to live if he did not instantly agree to it. M. le Duc d'Orleans returned to the sick man, and begged him so earnestly to do so, that he consented.

The operation was accordingly performed about five o'clock, and in five minutes, by La Peyronie, chief surgeon of the King, and successor to Marechal, who was present with Chirac and others of the most celebrated surgeons and doctors. The Cardinal cried and stormed strongly. M. le Duc d'Orleans returned into the chamber directly after the operation was performed, and the faculty did not dissimulate from him that, judging by the nature of the wound, and what had issued from it, the Cardinal had not long to live. He died, in fact, twenty-four hours afterwards, on the 10th, of August, at five o'clock in the morning, grinding his teeth against his surgeons and against Chirac, whom he had never ceased to abuse.

Extreme unction was, however, brought to him. Of the communion, nothing more was said—or of any priest for him—and he finished his life thus, in the utmost despair, and enraged at quitting it. Fortune had nicely played with him; slid made him dearly and slowly buy her favours by all sorts of trouble, care, projects, intrigues, fears, labour, torment; and at last showered down upon him torrents of greater power, unmeasured riches, to let him enjoy them only four years (dating from the time when he was made Secretary of State, and only two years dating from the time when he was made Cardinal and Prime Minister), and then snatched them from him, in the smiling moment when he was most enjoying them, at sixty- six years of age.

He died thus, absolute master of his master, less a prime minister than an all-powerful minister, exercising in full and undisturbed liberty the authority and the power of the King; he was superintendent of the post, Cardinal, Archbishop of Cambrai, had seven abbeys, with respect to which he was insatiable to the last; and he had set on foot overtures in order to seize upon those of Citeaux,

Premonte, and others, and it was averred that he received a pension from England of 40,000 livres sterling! I had the curiosity to ascertain his revenue, and I have thought what I found curious enough to be inserted here, diminishing some of the benefices to avoid all exaggeration. I have made a reduction, too, upon what he drew from his place of prime minister, and that of the post. I believe, also, that he had 20,000 livres from the clergy, as Cardinal, but I do not know it as certain. What he drew from Law was immense. He had made use of a good deal of it at Rome, in order to obtain his Cardinalship; but a prodigious sum of ready cash was left in his hands. He had an extreme quantity of the most beautiful plate in silver and enamel, most admirably worked; the richest furniture, the rarest jewels of all kinds, the finest and rarest horses of all countries, and the most superb equipages. His table was in every way exquisite and superb, and he did the honours of it very well, although extremely sober by nature and by regime.

The place of preceptor of M. le Duc d'Orleans had procured for him the
Abbey of Nogent-sous-Coucy; the marriage of the Prince that of Saint-
Just; his first journeys to Hanover and England, those of Airvause and of
Bourgueil: three other journeys, his omnipotence. What a monster of
Fortune! With what a commencement, and with what an end!

ACCOUNT OF HIS RICHES:

    Benefices ....324,000 livres
    Prime Minister and Past ....250,000 "
    Pension from England .... 960,000 "
                    — — — —
                1,534,000 "

On Wednesday evening, the day after his death, Dubois was carried from Versailles to the church of the chapter of Saint-Honore, in Paris, where he was interred some days after. Each of the academies of which he was a member had a service performed for him (at which they were present), the assembly of the clergy had another (he being their president); and as prime minister he had one at Notre Dame, at which the Cardinal de Noailles officiated, and at which the superior courts were present. There was no funeral oration at any of them. It could not be hazarded. His brother, more modest than he, and an honest man, kept the office of secretary of the cabinet, which he had, and which the Cardinal had given him. This brother found an immense heritage. He had but one son, canon of Saint-Honore, who had never desired places or livings, and who led a good life. He would touch scarcely anything of this rich succession. He employed a part of it in building for his uncle a sort of mausoleum (fine, but very modest, against the wall, at the end of the church, where the Cardinal is interred, with a Christian-like inscription), and distributed the rest to the poor, fearing lest this money should bring a curse upon him.

It was found some time after his death that the Cardinal had been long married, but very obscurely! He paid his wife to keep silent when he received his benefices; but when he dawned into greatness became much embarrassed with her. He was always in agony lest she should come forward and ruin him. His marriage had been made in Limousin, and celebrated in a village church. When he was named Archbishop of Cambrai he resolved to destroy the proofs of this marriage, and employed Breteuil, Intendant of Limoges, to whom he committed the secret, to do this for him skilfully and quietly.

Breteuil saw the heavens open before him if he could but succeed in this enterprise, so delicate and so important. He had intelligence, and knew how to make use of it. He goes to this village where the marriage had been celebrated, accompanied by only two or three valets, and arranges his journey so as to arrive at night, stops at the cure's house, in default of an inn, familiarly claims hospitality like a man surprised by the night, dying of hunger and thirst, and unable to go a step further.

The good cure; transported with gladness to lodge M. l'Intendant, hastily prepared all there was in the house, and had the honour of supping with him, whilst his servant regaled the two valets in another room, Breteuil having sent them all away in order to be alone with his host. Breteuil liked his glass and knew how to empty it. He pretended to find the supper good and the wine better. The cure, charmed with his guest, thought only of egging him on, as they say in the provinces. The tankard was on the table, and was drained again and again with a familiarity which transported the worthy priest. Breteuil; who had laid his project, succeeded in it, and made the good man so drunk that he could not keep upright, or see, or utter a word. When Breteuil had brought him to this state, and had finished him off with a few more draughts of wine, he profited by the information he had extracted from him during the first quarter of an hour of supper. He had asked if his registers were in good order, and how far they extended, and under pretext of safety against thieves, asked him where he kept them, and the keys of them, so that the moment Breteuil was certain the cure could no longer make use of his senses, he took his keys, opened the cupboard, took from it the register of the marriage of the year he wanted, very neatly detached the page he sought (and woe unto that marriage registered upon the same page), put it in his pocket, replaced the registers where he had found them, locked up the cupboard, and put back the keys in the place he had taken them from. His only thought after this was to steal off as soon as the dawn appeared, leaving the good cure snoring away the effects of the wine, and giving, some pistoles to the servant.

He went thence to the notary, who had succeeded to the business and the papers of the one who had made the contract of marriage; liked himself up with him, and by force and authority made him give up the minutes of the marriage contract. He sent afterwards for the wife of Dubois (from whose hands the wily Cardinal had already obtained the copy of the contract she possessed), threatened her with dreadful dungeons if she ever dared to breathe a word of her marriage, and promised marvels to her if she kept silent.

He assured her, moreover, that all she could say or do would be thrown away, because everything had been so arranged that she could prove nothing, and that if she dared to speak, preparations were made for condemning her as a calumniator and impostor, to rot with a shaven head in the prison of a convent! Breteuil placed these two important documents in the hands of Dubois, and was (to the surprise and scandal of all the world) recompensed, some time after, with the post of war secretary, which, apparently; he had done nothing to deserve, and for which he was utterly unqualified. The secret reason of his appointment was not discovered until long after.

Dubois' wife did not dare to utter a whisper. She came to Paris after the death of her husband. A good proportion was given to her of what was left. She lived obscure, but in easy circumstances, and died at Paris more than twenty years after the Cardinal Dubois, by whom she had had no children. The brother lived on very good terms with her. He was a village doctor when Dubois sent for him to Paris: In the end this history was known, and has been neither contradicted nor disavowed by anybody.

We have many examples of prodigious fortune acquired by insignificant people, but there is no example of a person so destitute of all talent (excepting that of low intrigue), as was Cardinal Dubois, being thus fortunate. His intellect was of the most ordinary kind; his knowledge the most common-place; his capacity nil; his exterior that of a ferret, of a pedant; his conversation disagreeable, broken, always uncertain; his falsehood written upon his forehead; his habits too measureless to be hidden; his fits of impetuosity resembling fits of madness; his head incapable of containing more than one thing at a time, and he incapable of following anything but his personal interest; nothing was sacred with him; he had no sort of worthy intimacy with any one; had a declared contempt for faith, promises, honour, probity, truth; took pleasure at laughing at all these things; was equally voluptuous and ambitious, wishing to be all in all in everything; counting himself alone as everything, and whatever was not connected with him as nothing; and regarding it as the height of madness to think or act otherwise. With all this he was soft, cringing, supple, a flatterer, and false admirer, taking all shapes with the greatest facility, and playing the most opposite parts in order to arrive at the different ends he proposed to himself; and nevertheless was but little capable of seducing. His judgment acted by fits and starts, was involuntarily crooked, with little sense or clearness; he was disagreeable in spite of himself. Nevertheless, he could be funnily vivacious when he wished, but nothing more, could tell a good story, spoiled, however, to some extent by his stuttering, which his falsehood had turned into a habit from the hesitation he always had in replying and in speaking. With such defects it is surprising that the only man he was able to seduce was M. le Duc d'Orleans, who had so much intelligence, such a well-balanced mind, and so much clear and rapid perception of character. Dubois gained upon him as a child while his preceptor; he seized upon him as a young man by favouring his liking for liberty, sham fashionable manners and debauchery, and his disdain of all rule. He ruined his heart, his mind, and his habits, by instilling into him the principles of libertines, which this poor prince could no more deliver himself from than from those ideas of reason, truth, and conscience which he always took care to stifle.

Dubois having insinuated himself into the favour of his master in this manner, was incessantly engaged in studying how to preserve his position. He never lost sight of his prince, whose great talents and great defects he had learnt how to profit by. The Regent's feebleness was the main rock upon which he built. As for Dubois' talent and capacity, as I have before said, they were worth nothing. All his success was due to his servile pliancy and base intrigues.

When he became the real master of the State he was just as incompetent as before. All his application was directed towards his master, and it had for sole aim that that master should not escape him. He wearied himself in watching all the movements of the prince, what he did, whom he saw, and for how long; his humour, his visage, his remarks at the issue of every audience and of every party; who took part in them, what was said and by whom, combining all these things; above all, he strove to frighten everybody from approaching the Regent, and kept no bounds with any one who had the temerity to do so without his knowledge and permission. This watching occupied all his days, and by it he regulated all his movements. This application, and the orders he was obliged to give for appearance sake, occupied all his time, so that he became inaccessible except for a few public audiences, or for others to the foreign ministers. Yet the majority of those ministers never could catch him, and were obliged to lie in wait for him upon staircases or in passages, where he did not expect to meet them. Once he threw into the fire a prodigious quantity of unopened letters, and then congratulated himself upon having got rid of all his business at once. At his death thousands of letters were found unopened.

Thus everything was in arrear, and nobody, not even the foreign ministers, dared to complain to M. le Duc d'Orleans, who, entirely abandoned to his pleasures, and always on the road from Versailles to Paris, never thought of business, only too satisfied to find himself so free, and attending to nothing except the few trifles he submitted to the King under the pretence of working with his Majesty. Thus, nothing could be settled, and all was in chaos. To govern in this manner there is no need for capacity. Two words to each minister charged with a department, and some care in garnishing the councils attended by the King, with the least important despatches (settling the others with M. le Duc d'Orleans) constituted all the labour of the prime minister; and spying, scheming, parade, flatteries, defence, occupied all his time. His fits of passion, full of insults and blackguardism, from which neither man nor woman, no matter of what rank, was sheltered, relieved him from an infinite number of audiences, because people preferred going to subalterns, or neglecting their business altogether, to exposing themselves to this fury and these affronts.

The mad freaks of Dubois, especially when he had become master, and thrown off all restraint, would fill a volume. I will relate only one or two as samples. His frenzy was such that he would sometimes run all round the chamber, upon the tables and chairs, without touching the floor! M. le Duc d'Orleans told me that he had often witnessed this.

Another sample:

The Cardinal de Gesvres came over to-day to complain to M. le Duc d'Orleans that the Cardinal Dubois had dismissed him in the most filthy terms. On a former occasion, Dubois had treated the Princesse de Montauban in a similar manner, and M. le Duc d'Orleans had replied to her complaints as he now replied to those of the Cardinal de Gesvres. He told the Cardinal, who was a man of good manners, of gravity, and of dignity (whereas the Princess deserved what she got) that he had always found the counsel of the Cardinal Dubois good, and that he thought he (Gesvres) would do well to follow the advice just given him! Apparently it was to free himself from similar complaints that he spoke thus; and, in fact, he had no more afterwards.

Another sample:

Madame de Cheverny, become a widow, had retired to the Incurables. Her place of governess of the daughters of M. le Duc d'Orleans had been given to Madame de Conflans. A little while after Dubois was consecrated, Madame la Duchesse d'Orleans asked Madame de Conflans if she had called upon him. Thereupon Madame de Conflans replied negatively and that she saw no reason for going, the place she held being so little mixed up in State affairs. Madame la Duchesse d'Orleans pointed out how intimate the Cardinal was with M. le Duc d'Orleans. Madame de Conflans still tried to back out, saying that he was a madman, who insulted everybody, and to whom she would not expose herself. She had wit and a tongue, and was supremely vain, although very polite. Madame la Duchesse d'Orleans burst out laughing at her fear, and said, that having nothing to ask of the Cardinal, but simply to render an account to him of the office M. le Duc d'Orleans had given her, it was an act of politeness which could only please him, and obtain for her his regard, far from having anything disagreeable, or to be feared about it; and finished by saying to her that it was proper, and that she wished her to go.

She went, therefore, for it was at Versailles, and arrived in a large cabinet, where there were eight or ten persons waiting to speak to the Cardinal, who was larking with one of his favourites, by the mantelpiece. Fear seized upon Madame de Conflans, who was little, and who appeared less. Nevertheless, she approached as this woman retired. The Cardinal, seeing her advance, sharply asked her what she wanted.

"Monseigneur," said she, — "Oh, Monseigneur — "

"Monseigneur," interrupted the Cardinal, "I can't now."

"But, Monseigneur," replied she —

"Now, devil take me, I tell you again," interrupted the Cardinal, "when I say I can't, I can't."

"Monseigneur," Madame de Conflans again said, in order to explain that she wanted nothing; but at this word the Cardinal seized her by the shoulders; and pushed her out, saying, "Go to the devil, and let me alone."

She nearly fell over, flew away in fury, weeping hot tears, and reached, in this state, Madame la Duchesse d'Orleans, to whom, through her sobs, she related the adventure.

People were so accustomed to the insults of the Cardinal, and this was thought so singular and so amusing, that the recital of it caused shouts of laughter, which finished off poor Madame de Conflans, who swore that, never in her life, would she put foot in the house of this madman.

The Easter Sunday after he was made Cardinal, Dubois woke about eight o'clock, rang his bells as though he would break them, called for his people with the most horrible blasphemies, vomited forth a thousand filthy expressions and insults, raved at everybody because he had not been awakened, said that he wanted to say mass, but knew not how to find time, occupied as he was. After this very beautiful preparation, he very wisely abstained from saying mass, and I don't know whether he ever did say it after his consecration.

He had taken for private secretary one Verrier, whom he had unfrocked from the Abbey of Saint-Germain-des-Pres, the business of which he had conducted for twenty years, with much cleverness and intelligence. He soon accommodated himself to the humours of the Cardinal, and said to him all he pleased.

One morning he was with the Cardinal, who asked for something that could not at once be found. Thereupon Dubois began to blaspheme, to storm against his clerks, saying that if he had not enough he would engage twenty, thirty, fifty, a hundred, and making the most frightful din. Verrier tranquilly listened to him. The Cardinal asked him if it was not a terrible thing to be so ill-served, considering the expense he was put to; then broke out again, and pressed him to reply.

"Monseigneur," said Verrier, "engage one more clerk, and give him, for sole occupation, to swear and storm for you, and all will go well; you will have much more time to yourself and will be better served."

The Cardinal burst out laughing, and was appeased.

Every evening he ate an entire chicken for his supper. I know not by whose carelessness, but this chicken was forgotten one evening by his people. As he was about to go to bed he bethought him of his bird, rang, cried out, stormed against his servants, who ran and coolly listened to him. Upon this he cried the more, and complained of not having been served. He was astonished when they replied to him that he had eaten his chicken, but that if he pleased they would put another down to the spit.

"What!" said he, "I have eaten my chicken!"

The bold and cool assertion of his people persuaded him, and they laughed at him.

I will say no more, because, I repeat it, volumes might be filled with these details. I have said enough to show what was this monstrous personage, whose death was a relief to great and little, to all Europe, even to his brother, whom he treated like a negro. He wanted to dismiss a groom on one occasion for having lent one of his coaches to this same brother, to go somewhere in Paris.

The most relieved of all was M. le Duc d'Orleans. For a long time he had groaned in secret beneath the weight of a domination so harsh, and of chains he had forged for himself. Not only he could no longer dispose or decide upon anything, but he could get the Cardinal to do nothing, great or small, he desired done. He was obliged, in everything, to follow the will of the Cardinal, who became furious, reproached him, and stormed at him when too much contradicted. The poor Prince felt thus the abandonment into which he had cast himself, and, by this abandonment, the power of the Cardinal, and the eclipse of his own power. He feared him; Dubois had become insupportable to him; he was dying with desire, as was shown in a thousand things, to get rid of him, but he dared not — he did not know how to set about it; and, isolated and unceasingly wretched as he was, there was nobody to whom he could unbosom himself; and the Cardinal, well informed of this, increased his freaks, so as to retain by fear what he had usurped by artifice, and what he no longer hoped to preserve in any other way.

As soon as Dubois was dead, M. le Duc d'Orleans returned to Meudon, to inform the King of the event. The King immediately begged him to charge himself with the management of public affairs, declared him prime minister, and received, the next day, his oath, the patent of which was immediately sent to the Parliament, and verified. This prompt declaration was caused by the fear Frejus had to see a private person prime minister. The King liked M. le Duc d'Orleans, as we have already seen by the respect he received from him, and by his manner of working with him. The Regent, without danger of being taken at his word, always left him master of all favours, and of the choice of persons he proposed to him; and, besides, never bothered him, or allowed business to interfere with his amusements. In spite of all the care and all the suppleness Dubois had employed in order to gain the spirit of the King, he never could succeed, and people remarked, without having wonderful eyes, a very decided repugnance of the King for him. The Cardinal was afflicted, but redoubled his efforts, in the hope at last of success. But, in addition to his own disagreeable manners, heightened by the visible efforts he made to please, he had two enemies near the King, very watchful to keep him away from the young prince — the Marechal de Villeroy, while he was there, and Frejus, who was much more dangerous, and who was resolved to overthrow him. Death, as we have seen, spared him the trouble.

The Court returned from Meudon to Paris on the 13th of August. Soon after I met M. le Duc d'Orleans there.

As soon as he saw me enter his cabinet he ran to me, and eagerly asked me if I meant to abandon him. I replied that while his Cardinal lived I felt I should be useless to him, but that now this obstacle was removed, I should always be very humbly at his service. He promised to live with me on the same terms as before, and, without a word upon the Cardinal, began to talk about home and foreign affairs. If I flattered myself that I was to be again of use to him for any length of time, events soon came to change the prospect. But I will not anticipate my story.

CHAPTER CXVI

The Duc de Lauzun died on the 19th of November, at the age of ninety years and six months. The intimate union of the two sisters I and he had espoused, and our continual intercourse at the Court (at Marly, we had a pavilion especially for us four), caused me to be constantly with him, and after the King's death we saw each other nearly every day at Paris, and unceasingly frequented each other's table. He was so extraordinary a personage, in every way so singular, that La Bruyere, with much justice, says of him in his "Characters," that others were not allowed to dream as he had lived. For those who saw him in his old age, this description seems even more just. That is what induces me to dwell upon him here. He was of the House of Caumont, the branch of which represented by the Ducs de la Force has always passed for the eldest, although that of Lauzun has tried to dispute with it.

The mother of M. de Lauzun was daughter of the Duc de la Force, son of the second Marechal Duc de la Force, and brother of the Marechale de Turenne, but by another marriage; the Marechale was by a first marriage. The father of M. de Lauzun was the Comte de Lauzun, cousin-german of the first Marechal Duc de Grammont, and of the old Comte de Grammont.

M. de Lauzun was a little fair man, of good figure, with a noble and expressively commanding face, but which was without charm, as I have heard people say who knew him when he was young. He was full of ambition, of caprice, of fancies; jealous of all; wishing always to go too far; never content with anything; had no reading, a mind in no way cultivated, and without charm; naturally sorrowful, fond of solitude, uncivilised; very noble in his dealings, disagreeable and malicious by nature, still more so by jealousy and by ambition; nevertheless, a good friend when a friend at all, which was rare; a good relative; enemy even of the indifferent; hard upon faults, and upon what was ridiculous, which he soon discovered; extremely brave, and as dangerously bold. As a courtier he was equally insolent and satirical, and as cringing as a valet; full of foresight, perseverance, intrigue, and meanness, in order to arrive at his ends; with this, dangerous to the ministers; at the Court feared by all, and full of witty and sharp remarks which spared nobody.

He came very young to the Court without any fortune, a cadet of Gascony, under the name of the Marquis de Puyguilhem. The Marechal de Grammont, cousin-german of his brother, lodged him: Grammont was then in high consideration at the Court, enjoyed the confidence of the Queen-mother, and of Cardinal Mazarin, and had the regiment of the guards and the reversion of it for the Comte de Guiche, his eldest son, who, the prince of brave fellows, was on his side in great favour with the ladies, and far advanced in the good graces of the King and of the Comtesse de Soissons, niece of the Cardinal, whom the King never quitted, and who was the Queen of the Court. This Comte de Guiche introduced to the Comtesse de Soissons the Marquis de Puyguilhem, who in a very little time became the King's favourite. The King, in fact, gave him his regiment of dragoons on forming it, and soon after made him Marechal de Camp, and created for him the post of colonel-general of dragoons.

The Duc de Mazarin, who in 1669 had already retired from the Court, wished to get rid of his post of grand master of the artillery; Puyguilhem had scent of his intention, and asked the King for this office. The King promised it to him, but on condition that he kept the matter secret some days. The day arrived on which the King had agreed to declare him. Puyguilhem, who had the entrees of the first gentleman of the chamber (which are also named the grandes entrees), went to wait for the King (who was holding a finance council), in a room that nobody entered during the council, between that in which all the Court waited, and that in which the council itself was held. He found there no one but Nyert, chief valet de chambre, who asked him how he happened to come there. Puyguilhem, sure of his affair, thought he should make a friend of this valet by confiding to him what was about to take place. Nyert expressed his joy; then drawing out his watch, said he should have time to go and execute a pressing commission the King had given him. He mounted four steps at a time the little staircase, at the head of which was the bureau where Louvois worked all day—for at Saint-Germain the lodgings were little and few—and the ministers and nearly all the Court lodged each at his own house in the town. Nyert entered the bureau of Louvois, and informed him that upon leaving the council (of which Louvois was not a member), the King was going to declare Puyguilhem grand master of the artillery, adding that he had just learned this news from Puyguilhem himself, and saying where he had left him.

Louvois hated Puyguilhem, friend of Colbert, his rival, and he feared his influence in a post which had so many intimate relations with his department of the war, the functions and authority of which he invaded as much as possible, a proceeding which he felt Puyguilhem was not the kind of man to suffer. He embraces Nyert, thanking him, dismisses him as quickly as possible, takes some papers to serve as an excuse, descends, and finds Puyguilhem and Nyert in the chamber, as above described. Nyert pretends to be surprised to see Louvois arrive, and says to him that the council has not broken up.

"No matter," replied Louvois, "I must enter, I have something important to say to the King;" and thereupon he enters. The King, surprised to see him, asks what brings him there, rises, and goes to him. Louvois draws him into the embrasure of a window, and says he knows that his Majesty is going to declare Puyguilhem grand master of the artillery; that he is waiting in the adjoining room for the breaking up of the council; that his Majesty is fully master of his favours and of his choice, but that he (Louvois) thinks it his duty to represent to him the incompatibility between Puyguilhem and him, his caprices, his pride; that he will wish to change everything in the artillery; that this post has such intimate relations with the war department, that continual quarrels will arise between the two, with which his Majesty will be importuned at every moment.

The King is piqued to see his secret known by him from whom, above all, he wished to hide it; he replies to Louvois, with a very serious air, that the appointment is not yet made, dismisses him, and reseats himself at the council. A moment after it breaks up. The King leaves to go to mass, sees Puyguilhem, and passes without saying anything to him. Puyguilhem, much astonished, waits all the rest of the day, and seeing that the promised declaration does not come, speaks of it to the King at night. The King replies to him that it cannot be yet, and that he will see; the ambiguity of the response, and the cold tone, alarm Puyguilhem; he is in favour with the ladies, and speaks the jargon of gallantry; he goes to Madame de Montespan, to whom he states his disquietude, and conjures her to put an end to it. She promises him wonders, and amuses him thus several days.

Tired of this, and not being able to divine whence comes his failure, he takes a resolution — incredible if it was not attested by all the Court of that time. The King was in the habit of visiting Madame de Montespan in the afternoon, and of remaining with her some time. Puyguilhem was on terms of tender intimacy with one of the chambermaids of Madame de Montespan. She privately introduced him into the room where the King visited Madame de Montespan, and he secreted himself under the bed. In this position he was able to hear all the conversation that took place between the King and his mistress above, and he learned by it that it was Louvois who had ousted him; that the King was very angry at the secret having got wind, and had changed his resolution to avoid quarrels between the artillery and the war department; and, finally, that Madame de Montespan, who had promised him her good offices, was doing him all the harm she could. A cough, the least movement, the slightest accident, might have betrayed the foolhardy Puyguilhem, and then what would have become of him? These are things the recital of which takes the breath away, and terrifies at the same time.

Puyguilhem was more fortunate than prudent, and was not discovered. The King and his mistress at last closed their conversation; the King dressed himself again, and went to his own rooms. Madame de Montespan went away to her toilette, in order to prepare for the rehearsal of a ballet to which the King, the Queen, and all the Court were going. The chambermaid drew Puyguilhem from under the bed, and he went and glued himself against the door of Madame de Montespan's chamber.

When Madame de Montespan came forth, in order to go to the rehearsal of the ballet, he presented his hand to her, and asked her, with an air of gentleness and of respect, if he might flatter himself that she had deigned to think of him when with the King. She assured him that she had not failed, and enumerated services she had; she said, just rendered him. Here and there he credulously interrupted her with questions, the better to entrap her; then, drawing near her, he told her she was a liar, a hussy, a harlot, and repeated to her, word for word, her conversation with the King!

Madame de Montespan was so amazed that she had not strength enough to reply one word; with difficulty she reached the place she was going to, and with difficulty overcame and hid the trembling of her legs and of her whole body; so that upon arriving at the room where the rehearsal was to take place, she fainted. All the Court was already there. The King, in great fright, came to her; it was not without much trouble she was restored to herself. The same evening she related to the King what had just happened, never doubting it was the devil who had so promptly and so precisely informed Puyguilhem of all that she had said to the King. The King was extremely irritated at the insult Madame de Montespan had received, and was much troubled to divine how Puyguilhem had been so exactly and so suddenly instructed.

Puyguilhem, on his side, was furious at losing the artillery, so that the King and he were under strange constraint together. This could last only a few days. Puyguilhem, with his grandes entrees, seized his opportunity and had a private audience with the King. He spoke to him of the artillery, and audaciously summoned him to keep his word. The King replied that he was not bound by it, since he had given it under secrecy, which he (Puyguilhem) had broken.

Upon this Puyguilhem retreats a few steps, turns his back upon the King, draws his sword, breaks the blade of it with his foot, and cries out in fury, that he will never in his life serve a prince who has so shamefully broken his word. The King, transported with anger, performed in that moment the finest action perhaps of his life. He instantly turned round, opened the window, threw his cane outside, said he should be sorry to strike a man of quality, and left the room.

The next morning, Puyguilhem, who had not dared to show himself since, was arrested in his chamber, and conducted to the Bastille. He was an intimate friend of Guitz, favourite of the King, for whom his Majesty had created the post of grand master of the wardrobe. Guitz had the courage to speak to the King in favour of Puyguilhem, and to try and reawaken the infinite liking he had conceived for the young Gascon. He succeeded so well in touching the King, by showing him that the refusal of such a grand post as the artillery had turned Puyguilhem's head, that his Majesty wished to make amends far this refusal. He offered the post of captain of the King's guards to Puyguilhem, who, seeing this incredible and prompt return of favour, re-assumed sufficient audacity to refuse it, flattering himself he should thus gain a better appointment. The King was not discouraged. Guitz went and preached to his friend in the Bastille, and with great trouble made him agree to have the goodness to accept the King's offer. As soon as he had accepted it he left the Bastille, went and saluted the King, and took the oaths of his new post, selling that which he occupied in the dragoons.

He had in 1665 the government of Berry, at the death of Marechal de Clerembault. I will not speak here of his adventures with Mademoiselle, which she herself so naively relates in her memoirs, or of his extreme folly in delaying his marriage with her (to which the King had consented), in order to have fine liveries, and get the marriage celebrated at the King's mass, which gave time to Monsieur (incited by M. le Prince) to make representations to the King, which induced him to retract his consent, breaking off thus the marriage. Mademoiselle made a terrible uproar, but Puyguilhem, who since the death of his father had taken the name of Comte de Lauzun, made this great sacrifice with good grace, and with more wisdom than belonged to him. He had the company of the hundred gentlemen, with battle-axes, of the King's household, which his father had had, and he had just been made lieutenant-general.

Lauzun was in love with Madame de Monaco, an intimate friend of Madame, and in all her Intrigues: He was very jealous of her, and was not pleased with her. One summer's afternoon he went to Saint-Cloud, and found Madame and her Court seated upon the ground, enjoying the air, and Madame de Monaco half lying down, one of her hands open and outstretched. Lauzun played the gallant with the ladies, and turned round so neatly that he placed his heel in the palm of Madame de Monaco, made a pirouette there, and departed. Madame de Monaco had strength enough to utter no cry, no word!

A short time after he did worse. He learnt that the King was on intimate terms with Madame de Monaco, learnt also the hour at which Bontems, the valet, conducted her, enveloped in a cloak, by a back staircase, upon the landing-place of which was a door leading into the King's cabinet, and in front of it a private cabinet. Lauzun anticipates the hour, and lies in ambush in the private cabinet, fastening it from within with a hook, and sees through the keyhole the King open the door of the cabinet, put the key outside (in the lock) and close the door again. Lauzun waits a little, comes out of his hiding-place, listens at the door in which the King had just placed the key, locks it, and takes out the key, which he throws into the private cabinet, in which he again shuts himself up.

Some time after Bontems and the lady arrive. Much astonished not to find the key in the door of the King's cabinet, Bontems gently taps at the door several times, but in vain; finally so loudly does he tap that the King hears the sound. Bontems says he is there, and asks his Majesty to open, because the key is not in the door. The King replies that he has just put it there. Bontems looks on the ground for it, the King meanwhile trying to open the door from the inside, and finding it double- locked. Of course all three are much astonished and much annoyed; the conversation is carried on through the door, and they cannot determine how this accident has happened. The King exhausts himself in efforts to force the door, in spite of its being double-locked. At last they are obliged to say good-bye through the door, and Lauzun, who hears every word they utter, and who sees them through the keyhole, laughs in his sleeve at their mishap with infinite enjoyment.

CHAPTER CXVII

In 1670 the King wished to make a triumphant journey with the ladies, under pretext of visiting his possessions in Flanders, accompanied by an army, and by all his household troops, so that the alarm was great in the Low Countries, which he took no pains to appease. He gave the command of all to Lauzun, with the patent of army-general. Lauzun performed the duties of his post with much intelligence, and with extreme gallantry and magnificence. This brilliancy, and this distinguished mark of favour, made Louvois, whom Lauzun in no way spared, think very seriously. He united with Madame de Montespan (who had not pardoned the discovery

Lauzun had made, or the atrocious insults he had bestowed upon her), and the two worked so well that they reawakened in the King's mind recollections of the broken sword, the refusal in the Bastille of the post of captain of the guards, and made his Majesty look upon Lauzun as a man who no longer knew himself, who had suborned Mademoiselle until he had been within an inch of marrying her, and of assuring to himself immense wealth; finally, as a man, very dangerous on account of his audacity, and who had taken it into his head to gain the devotion of the troops by his magnificence, his services to the officers, and by the manner in which he had treated them during the Flanders journey, making himself adored. They made him out criminal for having remained the friend of, and on terms of great intimacy with, the Comtesse de Soissons, driven from the Court and suspected of crimes. They must have accused Lauzun also of crimes which I have never heard of, in order to procure for him the barbarous treatment they succeeded in subjecting him to.

Their intrigues lasted all the year, 1671, without Lauzun discovering anything by the visage of the King, or that of Madame de Montespan. Both the King and his mistress treated him with their ordinary distinction and familiarity. He was a good judge of jewels (knowing also how to set them well), and Madame de Montespan often employed him in this capacity. One evening, in the middle of November, 1671, he arrived from Paris, where Madame de Montespan had sent him in the morning for some precious stones, and as he was about to enter his chamber he was arrested by the Marechal de Rochefort, captain of the guards.

Lauzun, in the utmost surprise, wished to know why, to see the King or Madame de Montespan—at least, to write to them; everything was refused him. He was taken to the Bastille, and shortly afterwards to Pignerol, where he was shut up in a low-roofed dungeon. His post of captain of the body-guard was given to M. de Luxembourg, and the government of Berry to the Duc de la Rochefoucauld, who, at the death of Guitz, at the passage of the Rhine, 12th June, 1672, was made grand master of the wardrobe.

It may be imagined what was the state of a man like Lauzun, precipitated, in a twinkling, from such a height to a dungeon in the chateau of Pignerol, without seeing anybody, and ignorant of his crime. He bore up, however, pretty well, but at last fell so ill that he began to think about confession. I have heard him relate that he feared a fictitious priest, and that, consequently, he obstinately insisted upon a Capuchin; and as soon as he came he seized him by the beard, and tugged at it, as hard as he could, on all sides, in order to see that it was not a sham one! He was four or five years in his gaol. Prisoners find employment which necessity teaches them. There ware prisoners above him and at the side of him. They found means to speak to him. This intercourse led them to make a hole, well hidden, so as to talk more easily; then to increase it, and visit each other.

The superintendent Fouquet had been enclosed near them ever since December, 1664. He knew by his neighbours (who had found means of seeing him) that Lauzun was under them. Fouquet, who received no news, hoped for some from him, and had a great desire to see him. He, had left Lauzun a young man, dawning at the Court, introduced by the Marechal de Grammont, well received at the house of the Comtesse de Soissons, which the King never quitted, and already looked upon favourably. The prisoners, who had become intimate with Lauzun, persuaded him to allow himself to be drawn up through their hole, in order to see Fouquet in their dungeon. Lauzun was very willing. They met, and Lauzun began relating, accordingly, his fortunes and his misfortunes, to Fouquet. The unhappy superintendent opened wide his ears and eyes when he heard this young Gasepan (once only too happy to be welcomed and harboured by the Marechal de Grammont) talk of having been general of dragoons, captain of the guards, with the patent and functions of army-general! Fouquet no longer knew where he was, believed Lauzun mad, and that he was relating his visions, when he described how he had missed the artillery, and what had passed afterwards thereupon: but he was convinced that madness had reached its climax, and was afraid to be with Lauzun, when he heard him talk of his marriage with Mademoiselle, agreed to by the King, how broken, and the wealth she had assured to him. This much curbed their intercourse, as far as Fouquet was concerned, for he, believing the brain of Lauzun completely turned, took for fairy tales all the stories the Gascon told him of what had happened in the world, from the imprisonment of the one to the imprisonment of the other.

The confinement of Fouquet was a little relieved before that of Lauzun. His wife and some officers of the chateau of Pignerol had permission to see him, and to tell him the news of the day. One of the first things he did was to tell them of this poor Puyguilhem, whom he had left young, and on a tolerably good footing for his age, at the Court, and whose head was now completely turned, his madness hidden within the prison walls; but what was his astonishment when they all assured him that what he had heard was perfectly true! He did not return to the subject, and was tempted to believe them all mad together. It was some time before he was persuaded.

In his turn, Lauzun was taken from his dungeon, and had a chamber, and soon after had the same liberty that had been given to Fouquet; finally, they were allowed to see each other as much as they liked. I have never known what displeased Lauzun, but he left Pignerol the enemy of Fouquet, and did him afterwards all the harm he could, and after his death extended his animosity to his family.

During the long imprisonment of Lauzun, Madame de Nogent, one of his sisters, took such care of his revenues that he left Pignerol extremely rich.

Mademoiselle, meanwhile, was inconsolable at this long and harsh imprisonment, and took all possible measures to deliver Lauzun. The King at last resolved to turn this to the profit of the Duc du Maine, and to make Mademoiselle pay dear for the release of her lover. He caused a proposition to be made to her, which was nothing less than to assure to the Duc du Maine, and his posterity after her death, the countdom of Eu, the Duchy of Aumale, and the principality of Domfes! The gift was enormous, not only as regards the value, but the dignity and extent of these three slices. Moreover, she had given the first two to Lauzun, with the Duchy of Saint-Forgeon, and the fine estate of Thiers, in Auvergne, when their marriage was broken off, and she would have been obliged to make him renounce Eu and Aumale before she could have disposed of them in favour of the Duc du Maine. Mademoiselle could not, make up her mind to this yoke, or to strip Lauzun of such considerable benefits. She was importuned to the utmost, finally menaced by the ministers, now Louvois, now Colbert. With the latter she was better pleased, because he had always been on good terms with Lauzun, and because he handled her more gently than Louvois, who, an enemy of her lover, always spoke in the harshest terms. Mademoiselle unceasingly felt that the King did not like her, and that he had never pardoned her the Orleans journey, still less her doings at the Bastille, when she fired its cannons upon the King's troops, and saved thus M. le Prince and his people, at the combat of the Faubourg Saint-Antoine. Feeling, therefore, that the King, hopelessly estranged from her, and consenting to give liberty to Lauzun only from his passion for elevating and enriching his bastards, would not cease to persecute her until she had consented — despairing of better terms, she agreed to the gift, with the most bitter tears and complaints. But it was found that, in order to make valid the renunciation of Lauzun, he must be set at liberty, so that it was pretended he had need of the waters of Bourbon, and Madame de Montespan also, in order that they might confer together upon this affair.

Lauzun was taken guarded to Bourbon by a detachment of musketeers, commanded by Maupertuis. Lauzun saw Madame de Montespan at Bourbon; but he was so indignant at the terms proposed to him as the condition of his liberty, that after long disputes he would hear nothing more on the subject, and was reconducted to Pignerol as he had been brought.

This firmness did not suit the King, intent upon the fortune of his well- beloved bastard. He sent Madame de Nogent to Pignerol; then Borin (a friend of Lauzun, and who was mixed up in all his affairs), with menaces and promises. Borin, with great trouble, obtained the consent of Lauzun, and brought about a second journey to Bourbon for him and Madame de Montespan, with the same pretext of the waters. Lauzun was conducted there as before, and never pardoned Maupertuis the severe pedantry of his exactitude. This last journey was made in the autumn of 1680. Lauzun consented to everything. Madame de Montespan returned triumphant. Maupertuis and his musketeers took leave of Lauzun at Bourbon, whence he had permission to go and reside at Angers; and immediately after, this exile was enlarged, so that he had the liberty of all Anjou and Lorraine.

The consummation of the affair was deferred until the commencement of February, 1681, in order to give him a greater air of liberty. Thus Lauzun had from Mademoiselle only Saint-Forgeon and Thiers, after having been on the point of marrying her, and of succeeding to all her immense wealth. The Duc du Maine was instructed to make his court to Mademoiselle, who always received him very coldly, and who saw him take her arms, with much vexation, as a mark of his gratitude, in reality for the Sake of the honour it brought him; for the arms were those of Gaston, which the Comte de Toulouse afterwards took, not for the same reason, but under pretext of conformity with his brother; and they have handed them down to their children.

Lauzun, who had been led to expect much more gentle treatment, remained four years in these two provinces, of which he grew as weary as was Mademoiselle at his absence. She cried out in anger against Madame de Montespan and her son; complained loudly that after having been so pitilessly fleeced, Lauzun was still kept removed from her; and made such a stir that at last she obtained permission for him to return to Paris, with entire liberty; on condition, however, that he did not approach within two leagues of any place where the King might be.

Lauzun came, therefore, to Paris, and assiduously visited his benefactors. The weariness of this kind of exile, although so softened, led him into high play, at which he was extremely successful; always a good and sure player, and very straightforward, he gained largely. Monsieur, who sometimes made little visits to Paris, and who played very high, permitted him to join the gambling parties of the Palais Royal, then those of Saint-Cloud. Lauzun passed thus several years, gaining and lending much money very nobly; but the nearer he found himself to the Court, and to the great world, the more insupportable became to him the prohibition he had received.

Finally, being no longer able to bear it, he asked the King for permission to go to England, where high play was much in vogue. He obtained it, and took with him a good deal of money, which secured him an open-armed reception in London, where he was not less successful than in Paris.

James II., then reigning, received Lauzun with distinction. But the Revolution was already brewing. It burst after Lauzun had been in England eight or ten months. It seemed made expressly for him, by the success he derived from it, as everybody is aware. James II., no longer knowing what was to become of him—betrayed by his favourites and his ministers, abandoned by all his nation, the Prince of Orange master of all hearts, the troops, the navy, and ready to enter London—the unhappy monarch confided to Lauzun what he held most dear—the Queen and the Prince of Wales, whom Lauzun happily conducted to Calais. The Queen at once despatched a courier to the King, in the midst of the compliments of which she insinuated that by the side of her joy at finding herself and her son in security under his protection, was her grief at not daring to bring with her him to whom she owed her safety.

The reply of the King, after much generous and gallant sentiment, was, that he shared this obligation with her, and that he hastened to show it to her, by restoring the Comte de Lauzun to favour.

In effect, when the Queen presented Lauzun to the King, in the Palace of Saint-Germain (where the King, with all the family and all the Court, came to meet her), he treated him as of old, gave him the privilege of the grandes entrees, and promised him a lodging at Versailles, which he received immediately after. From that day he always went to Marly, and to Fontainebleau, and, in fact, never after quitted the Court. It may be imagined what was the delight of such an ambitious courtier, so completely re-established in such a sudden and brilliant manner. He had also a lodging in the chateau of Saint-Germain, chosen as the residence of this fugitive Court, at which King James soon arrived.

Lauzun, like a skilful courtier, made all possible use of the two Courts, and procured for himself many interviews with the King, in which he received minor commissions. Finally, he played his cards so well that the King permitted him to receive in Notre Dame, at Paris, the Order of the Garter, from the hands of the King of England, accorded to him at his second passage into Ireland the rank of lieutenant-general of his auxiliary army, and permitted at the same time that he should be of the staff of the King of England, who lost Ireland during the same campaign at the battle of the Boyne. He returned into France with the Comte de Lauzun, for whom he obtained letters of the Duke; which were verified at the Parliament in May, 1692. What a miraculous return of fortune! But what a fortune, in comparison with that of marrying Mademoiselle, with the donation of all her prodigious wealth, and the title and dignity of Duke and Peer of Montpensier. What a monstrous pedestal! And with children by this marriage, what a flight might not Lauzun have taken, and who can say where he might have arrived?

CHAPTER CXVIII

I have elsewhere related Lauzun's humours, his notable wanton tricks, and his rare singularity.

He enjoyed, during the rest of his long life, intimacy with the King, distinction at the Court, great consideration, extreme abundance, kept up the state of a great nobleman, with one of the most magnificent houses of the Court, and the best table, morning and evening, most honourably frequented, and at Paris the same, after the King's death: All this did not content him. He could only approach the King with outside familiarity; he felt that the mind and the heart of that monarch were on their guard against him, and in an estrangement that not all his art nor all his application could ever overcome. This is what made him marry my sister-in-law, hoping thus to re-establish himself in serious intercourse with the King by means of the army that M. le Marechal de Lorge commanded in Germany; but his project failed, as has been seen. This is what made him bring about the marriage of the Duc de Lorge with the daughter of Chamillart, in order to reinstate himself by means of that ministry; but without success. This is what made him undertake the journey to Aix- la-Chapelle, under the pretext of the waters, to obtain information which might lead to private interviews with the King, respecting the peace; but he was again unsuccessful. All his projects failed; in fact, he unceasingly sorrowed, and believed himself in profound disgrace—even saying so. He left nothing undone in order to pay his court, at bottom with meanness, but externally with dignity; and he every year celebrated a sort of anniversary of his disgrace, by extraordinary acts, of which ill-humour and solitude were oftentimes absurdly the fruit. He himself spoke of it, and used to say that he was not rational at the annual return of this epoch, which was stronger than he. He thought he pleased the King by this refinement of attention, without perceiving he was laughed at.

By nature he was extraordinary in everything, and took pleasure in affecting to be more so, even at home, and among his valets. He counterfeited the deaf and the blind, the better to see and hear without exciting suspicion, and diverted himself by laughing at fools, even the most elevated, by holding with them a language which had no sense. His manners were measured, reserved, gentle, even respectful; and from his low and honeyed tongue, came piercing remarks, overwhelming by their justice, their force, or their satire, composed of two or three words, perhaps, and sometimes uttered with an air of naivete or of distraction, as though he was not thinking of what he said. Thus he was feared, without exception, by everybody, and with many acquaintances he had few or no friends, although he merited them by his ardor in seeing everybody as much as he could, and by his readiness in opening his purse. He liked to gather together foreigners of any distinction, and perfectly did the honours of the Court. But devouring ambition poisoned his life; yet he was a very good and useful relative.

During the summer which followed the death of Louis XIV. there was a review of the King's household troops, led by M. le Duc d'Orleans, in the plain by the side of the Bois de Boulogne. Passy, where M. de Lauzun had a pretty house, is on the other side. Madame de Lauzun was there with company, and I slept there the evening before the review. Madame de Poitiers, a young widow, and one of our relatives, was there too, and was dying to see the review, like a young person who has seen nothing, but who dares not show herself in public in the first months of her mourning.

How she could be taken was discussed in the company, and it was decided that Madame de Lauzun could conduct her a little way, buried in her carriage. In the midst of the gaiety of this party, M. de Lauzun arrived from Paris, where he had gone in the morning. He was told what had just been decided. As soon as he learnt it he flew into a fury, was no longer master of himself, broke off the engagement, almost foaming at the mouth; said the most disagreeable things to his wife in the strongest, the harshest, the most insulting, and the most foolish terms. She gently wept; Madame de Poitiers sobbed outright, and all the company felt the utmost embarrassment. The evening appeared an age, and the saddest refectory repast a gay meal by the side of our supper. He was wild in the midst of the profoundest silence; scarcely a word was said. He quitted the table, as usual, at the fruit, and went to bed. An attempt was made to say something afterwards by way of relief, but Madame de Lauzun politely and wisely stopped the conversation, and brought out cards in order to turn the subject.

The next morning I went to M. de Lauzun, in order to tell him in plain language my opinion of the scene of the previous evening. I had not the time. As soon as he saw me enter he extended his arms, and cried that I saw a madman, who did not deserve my visit, but an asylum; passed the strongest eulogies upon his wife (which assuredly she merited), said he was not worthy of her, and that he ought to kiss the ground upon which she walked; overwhelmed himself with blame; then, with tears in his eyes, said he was more worthy of pity than of anger; that he must admit to me all his shame and misery; that he was more than eighty years of age; that he had neither children nor survivors; that he had been captain of the guards; that though he might be so again, he should be incapable of the function; that he unceasingly said this to himself, and that yet with all this he could not console himself for having been so no longer during the many years since he had lost his post; that he had never been able to draw the dagger from his heart; that everything which recalled the memory of the past made him beside himself, and that to hear that his wife was going to take Madame de Poitiers to see a review of the body-guards, in which he now counted for nothing, had turned his head, and had rendered him wild to the extent I had seen; that he no longer dared show himself before any one after this evidence of madness; that he was going to lock himself up in his chamber, and that he threw himself at my feet in order to conjure me to go and find his wife, and try to induce her to take pity on and pardon a senseless old man, who was dying with grief and shame. This admission, so sincere and so dolorous to make, penetrated me. I sought only to console him and compose him. The reconciliation was not difficult; we drew him from his chamber, not without trouble, and he evinced during several days as much disinclination to show himself, as I was told, for I went away in the evening, my occupations keeping me very busy.

I have often reflected, apropos of this, upon the extreme misfortune of allowing ourselves to be carried away by the intoxication of the world, and into the formidable state of an ambitious man, whom neither riches nor comfort, neither dignity acquired nor age, can satisfy, and who, instead of tranquilly enjoying what he possesses, and appreciating the happiness of it, exhausts himself in regrets, and in useless and continual bitterness. But we die as we have lived, and 'tis rare it happens otherwise. This madness respecting the captaincy of the guards so cruelly dominated M. de Lauzun, that he often dressed himself in a blue coat, with silver lace, which, without being exactly the uniform of the captain of, the body-guards, resembled it closely, and would have rendered him ridiculous if he had not accustomed people to it, made himself feared, and risen above all ridicule.

With all his scheming and cringing he fell foul of everybody, always saying some biting remark with dove-like gentleness. Ministers, generals, fortunate people and their families, were the most ill-treated. He had, as it were, usurped the right of saying and doing what he pleased; nobody daring to be angry with him. The Grammonts alone were excepted. He always remembered the hospitality and the protection he had received from them at the outset of his life. He liked them; he interested himself in them; he was in respect before them. Old Comte Grammont took advantage of this and revenged the Court by the sallies he constantly made against Lauzun, who never returned them or grew angry, but gently avoided him. He always did a good deal for the children of his sisters.

During the plague the Bishop of Marseilles had much signalised himself by wealth spent and danger incurred. When the plague had completely passed away, M. de Lauzun asked M. le Duc d'Orleans for an abbey for the Bishop. The Regent gave away some livings soon after, and forgot M. de Marseilles. Lauzun pretended to be ignorant of it, and asked M. le Duc d'Orleans if he had had the goodness to remember him. The Regent was embarrassed. The Duc de Lauzun, as though to relieve him from his embarrassment, said, in a gentle and respectful tone, "Monsieur, he will do better another time," and with this sarcasm rendered the Regent dumb, and went away smiling. The story got abroad, and M. le Duc d'Orleans repaired his forgetfulness by the bishopric of Laon, and upon the refusal of M. de Marseilles to change, gave him a fat abbey.

M. de Lauzun hindered also a promotion of Marshal of France by the ridicule he cast upon the candidates. He said to the Regent, with that gentle and respectful tone he knew so well how to assume, that in case any useless Marshals of France (as he said) were made, he begged his Royal Highness to remember that he was the oldest lieutenant-general of the realm, and that he had had the honour of commanding armies with the patent of general. I have elsewhere related other of his witty remarks. He could not keep them in; envy and jealousy urged him to utter them, and as his bon-mots always went straight to the point, they were always much repeated.

We were on terms of continual intimacy; he had rendered me real solid friendly services of himself, and I paid him all sorts of respectful attentions, and he paid me the same. Nevertheless, I did not always escape his tongue; and on one occasion, he was perhaps within an inch of doing me much injury by it.

The King (Louis XIV.) was declining; Lauzun felt it, and began to think of the future. Few people were in favour with M. le Duc d'Orleans; nevertheless, it was seen that his grandeur was approaching. All eyes were upon him, shining with malignity, consequently upon me, who for a long time had been the sole courtier who remained publicly attached to him, the sole in his confidence. M. de Lauzun came to dine at my house, and found us at table. The company he saw apparently displeased him; for he went away to Torcy, with whom I had no intimacy, and who was also at table, with many people opposed to M. le Duc d'Orleans, Tallard, among others, and Tesse.

"Monsieur," said Lauzun to Torcy, with a gentle and timid air, familiar to him, "take pity upon me, I have just tried to dine with M. de Saint- Simon. I found him at table, with company; I took care not to sit down with them, as I did not wish to be the 'zeste' of the cabal. I have come here to find one."

They all burst out laughing. The remark instantly ran over all Versailles. Madame de Maintenon and M. du Maine at once heard it, and nevertheless no sign was anywhere made. To have been angry would only have been to spread it wider: I took the matter as the scratch of an ill- natured cat, and did not allow Lauzun to perceive that I knew it.

Two or three years before his death he had an illness which reduced him to extremity. We were all very assiduous, but he would see none of us, except Madame de Saint-Simon, and her but once. Languet, cure of Saint- Sulpice, often went to him, and discoursed most admirably to him. One day, when he was there, the Duc de la Force glided into the chamber: M. de Lauzun did not like him at all, and often laughed at him. He received him tolerably well, and continued to talk aloud with the cure.

Suddenly he turned to the cure, complimented and thanked him, said he had nothing more valuable to give him than his blessing, drew his arm from the bed, pronounced the blessing, and gave it to him. Then turning to the Duc de la Force, Lauzun said he had always loved and respected him as the head of his house, and that as such he asked him for his blessing.

These two men, the cure and the Duc de la Force, were astonished, could not utter a word. The sick man redoubled his instances. M. de la Force, recovering himself, found the thing so amusing, that he gave his blessing; and in fear lest he should explode, left the room, and came to us in the adjoining chamber, bursting with laughter, and scarcely able to relate what had happened to him.

A moment after, the cure came also, all abroad, but smiling as much as possible, so as to put a good face on the matter. Lauzun knew that he was ardent and skilful in drawing money from people for the building of a church, and had often said he would never fall into his net; he suspected that the worthy cure's assiduities had an interested motive, and laughed at him in giving him only his blessing (which he ought to have received from him), and in perseveringly asking the Duc de la Force for his. The cure, who saw the point of the joke, was much mortified, but, like a sensible man, he was not less frequent in his visits to M. de Lauzun after this; but the patient cut short his visits, and would not understand the language he spoke.

Another day, while he was still very ill, Biron and his wife made bold to enter his room on tiptoe, and kept behind his curtains, out of sight, as they thought; but he perceived them by means of the glass on the chimney- piece. Lauzun liked Biron tolerably well, but Madame Biron not at all; she was, nevertheless, his niece, and his principal heiress; he thought her mercenary, and all her manners insupportable to him. In that he was like the rest of the world. He was shocked by this unscrupulous entrance into his chamber, and felt that, impatient for her inheritance, she came in order to make sure of it, if he should die directly. He wished to make her repent of this, and to divert himself at her expense. He begins, therefore; to utter aloud, as though believing himself alone, an ejaculatory orison, asking pardon of God for his past life, expressing himself as though persuaded his death was nigh, and saying that, grieved at his inability to do penance, he wishes at least to make use of all the wealth he possesses, in order to redeem his sins, and bequeath that wealth to the hospitals without any reserve; says it is the sole road to salvation left to him by God, after having passed a long life without thinking of the future; and thanks God for this sole resource left him, which he adopts with all his heart!

He accompanied this resolution with a tone so touched, so persuaded, so determined, that Biron and his wife did not doubt for a moment he was going to execute his design, or that they should be deprived of all the succession. They had no desire to spy any more, and went, confounded, to the Duchesse de Lauzun, to relate to her the cruel decree they had just heard pronounced, conjuring her to try and moderate it. Thereupon the patient sent for the notaries, and Madame Biron believed herself lost. It was exactly the design of the testator to produce this idea. He made the notaries wait; then allowed them to enter, and dictated his will, which was a death-blow to Madame de Biron. Nevertheless, he delayed signing it, and finding himself better and better, did not sign it at all. He was much diverted with this farce, and could not restrain his laughter at it, when reestablished. Despite his age, and the gravity of his illness, he was promptly cured and restored to his usual health.

He was internally as strong as a lion, though externally very delicate. He dined and supped very heartily every day of an excellent and very delicate cheer, always with good company, evening and morning; eating of everything, 'gras' and 'maigre', with no choice except that of his taste and no moderation. He took chocolate in the morning, and had always on the table the fruits in season, and biscuits; at other times beer, cider, lemonade, and other similar drinks iced; and as he passed to and fro, ate and drank at this table every afternoon, exhorting others to do the same. In this way he left table or the fruit, and immediately went to bed.

I recollect that once, among others, he ate at my house, after his illness, so much fish, vegetables, and all sorts of things (I having no power to hinder him), that in the evening we quietly sent to learn whether he had not felt the effects of them. He was found at table eating with good appetite.

His gallantry was long faithful to him. Mademoiselle was jealous of it, and that often controlled him. I have heard Madame de Fontenelles (a very enviable woman, of much intelligence, very truthful, and of singular virtue), I have heard her say, that being at Eu with Mademoiselle, M. de Lauzun came there and could not desist from running after the girls; Mademoiselle knew it, was angry, scratched him, and drove him from her presence. The Comtesse de Fiesque reconciled them. Mademoiselle appeared at the end of a long gallery; Lauzun was at the other end, and he traversed the whole length of it on his knees until he reached the feet of Mademoiselle. These scenes, more or less moving, often took place afterwards. Lauzun allowed himself to be beaten, and in his turn soundly beat Mademoiselle; and this happened several times, until at last, tired of each other, they quarrelled once for all and never saw each other again; he kept several portraits of her, however, in his house or upon him, and never spoke of her without much respect. Nobody doubted they had been secretly married. At her death he assumed a livery almost black, with silver lace; this he changed into white with a little blue upon gold, when silver was prohibited upon liveries.

His temper, naturally scornful and capricious, rendered more so by prison and solitude, had made him a recluse and dreamer; so that having in his house the best of company, he left them to Madame de Lauzun, and withdrew alone all the afternoon, several hours running, almost always without books, for he read only a few works of fancy—a very few—and without sequence; so that he knew nothing except what he had seen, and until the last was exclusively occupied with the Court and the news of the great world. I have a thousand times regretted his radical incapacity to write down what he had seen and done. It would have been a treasure of the most curious anecdotes, but he had no perseverance, no application. I have often tried to draw from him some morsels. Another misfortune. He began to relate; in the recital names occurred of people who had taken part in what he wished to relate. He instantly quitted the principal object of the story in order to hang on to one of these persons, and immediately after to some other person connected with the first, then to a third, in the manner of the romances; he threaded through a dozen histories at once, which made him lose ground and drove him from one to the other without ever finishing anything; and with this his words were very confused, so that it was impossible to learn anything from him or retain anything he said. For the rest, his conversation was always constrained by caprice or policy; and was amusing only by starts, and by the malicious witticisms which sprung out of it. A few months after his last illness, that is to say, when he was more than ninety years of age, he broke in his horses and made a hundred passades at the Bois de Boulogne (before the King, who was going to the Muette), upon a colt he had just trained, surprising the spectators by his address, his firmness, and his grace. These details about him might go on for ever.

His last illness came on without warning, almost in a moment, with the most horrible of all ills, a cancer in the mouth. He endured it to the last with incredible patience and firmness, without complaint, without spleen, without the slightest repining; he was insupportable to himself. When he saw his illness somewhat advanced, he withdrew into a little apartment (which he had hired with this object in the interior of the Convent of the Petits Augustins, into which there was an entrance from his house) to die in repose there, inaccessible to Madame de Biron and every other woman, except his wife, who had permission to go in at all hours, followed by one of her attendants.

Into this retreat Lauzun gave access only to his nephews and brothers-in- law, and to them as little as possible. He thought only of profiting by his terrible state, of giving all his time to the pious discourses of his confessor and of some of the pious people of the house, and to holy reading; to everything, in fact, which best could prepare him for death. When we saw him, no disorder, nothing lugubrious, no trace of suffering, politeness, tranquillity, conversation but little animated, indifference to what was passing in the world, speaking of it little and with difficulty; little or no morality, still less talk of his state; and this uniformity, so courageous and so peaceful, was sustained full four months until the end; but during the last ten or twelve days he would see neither brothers-in-law nor nephews, and as for his wife, promptly dismissed her. He received all the sacraments very edifyingly, and preserved his senses to the last moment: The morning of the day during the night of which he died, he sent for Biron, said he had done for him all that Madame de Lauzun had wished; that by his testament he gave him all his wealth, except a trifling legacy to the son of his other sister, and some recompenses to his domestics; that all he had done for him since his marriage, and what he did in dying, he (Biron) entirely owed to Madame de Lauzun; that he must never forget the gratitude he owed her; that he prohibited him, by the authority of uncle and testator, ever to cause her any trouble or annoyance, or to have any process against her, no matter of what kind. It was Biron himself who told me this the next day, in the terms I have given. M. de Lauzun said adieu to him in a firm tone, and dismissed him. He prohibited, and reasonably, all ceremony; he was buried at the Petits Augustins; he had nothing from the King but the ancient company of the battle-axes, which was suppressed two days after. A month before his death he had sent for Dillon (charged here with the affairs of King James, and a very distinguished officer general), to whom he surrendered his collar of the Order of the Garter, and a George of onyx, encircled with perfectly beautiful and large diamonds, to be sent back to the Prince.

I perceive at last, that I have been very prolix upon this man, but the extraordinary singularity of his life, and my close connexion with him, appear to me sufficient excuses for making him known, especially as he did not sufficiently figure in general affairs to expect much notice in the histories that will appear. Another sentiment has extended my recital. I am drawing near a term I fear to reach, because my desires cannot be in harmony with the truth; they are ardent, consequently gainful, because the other sentiment is terrible, and cannot in any way be palliated; the terror of arriving there has stopped me—nailed me where I was—frozen me.

It will easily be seen that I speak of the death (and what a death!) of M. le Duc d'Orleans; and this frightful recital, especially after such a long attachment (it lasted all his life, and will last all mine), penetrates me with terror and with grief for him. The Regent had said, when he died he should like to die suddenly: I shudder to my very marrow, with the horrible suspicion that God, in His anger, granted his desire.

CHAPTER CXIX

The new chateau of Meudon, completely furnished, had been restored to me since the return of the Court to Versailles, just as I had had it before the Court came to Meudon. The Duc and Duchesse d'Humieres were with us there, and good company. One morning towards the end of October, 1723, the Duc d'Humieres wished me to conduct him to Versailles, to thank M. le Duc d'Orleans.

We found the Regent dressing in the vault he used as his wardrobe. He was upon his chair among his valets, and one or two of his principal officers. His look terrified me. I saw a man with hanging head, a purple-red complexion, and a heavy stupid air. He did not even see me approach. His people told him. He slowly turned his head towards me, and asked me with a thick tongue what brought me. I told him. I had intended to pass him to come into the room where he dressed himself, so as not to keep the Duc d'Humieres waiting; but I was so astonished that I stood stock still.

I took Simiane, first gentleman of his chamber, into a window, and testified to him my surprise and my fear at the state in which I saw M. le Duc d'Orleans.

Simiane replied that for a long time he had been so in the morning; that to-day there was nothing extraordinary about him, and that I was surprised simply because I did not see him at those hours; that nothing would be seen when he had shaken himself a little in dressing. There was still, however, much to be seen when he came to dress himself. The Regent received the thanks of the Duc d'Humieres with an astonished and heavy air; he who always was so gracious and so polite to everybody, and who so well knew how to express himself, scarcely replied to him! A moment after, M. d'Humieres and I withdrew. We dined with the Duc de Gesvres, who led him to the King to thank his Majesty.

The condition of M. le Duc d'Orleans made me make many reflections. For a very long time the Secretaries of State had told me that during the first hours of the morning they could have made him pass anything they wished, or sign what might have been the most hurtful to him. It was the fruit of his suppers. Within the last year he himself had more than once told me that Chirac doctored him unceasingly, without effect; because he was so full that he sat down to table every evening without hunger, without any desire to eat, though he took nothing in the morning, and simply a cup of chocolate between one and two o'clock in the day (before everybody), it being then the time to see him in public. I had not kept dumb with him thereupon, but all my representations were perfectly useless. I knew moreover, that Chirac had continually told him that the habitual continuance of his suppers would lead him to apoplexy, or dropsy on the chest, because his respiration was interrupted at times; upon which he had cried out against this latter malady, which was a slow, suffocating, annoying preparation for death, saying that he preferred apoplexy, which surprised and which killed at once, without allowing time to think of it!

Another man, instead of crying out against this kind of death with which he was menaced, and of preferring another, allowing him no time for reflection, would have thought about leading a sober, healthy, and decent life, which, with the temperament he had, would have procured him a very long time, exceeding agreeable in the situation—very probably durable— in which he found himself; but such was the double blindness of this unhappy prince.

I was on terms of much intimacy with M. de Frejus, and since, in default of M. le Duc d'Orleans, there must be another master besides the King, until he could take command, I preferred this prelate to any other. I went to him, therefore, and told him what I had seen this morning of the state of M. le Duc d'Orleans. I predicted that his death must soon come, and that it would arrive suddenly, without warning. I counselled Frejus, therefore, to have all his arrangements ready with the King, in order to fill up the Regent's place of prime minister when it should become vacant. M. de Frejus appeared very grateful for the advice, but was measured and modest as though he thought the post much above him!

On the 22nd of December, 1723, I went from Meudon to Versailles to see M. le Duc d'Orleans; I was three-quarters of an hour with him in his cabinet, where I had found him alone. We walked to and fro there, talking of affairs of which he was going to give an account to the King that day. I found no difference in him, his state was, as usual, languid and heavy, as it had been for some time, but his judgment was clear as ever. I immediately returned to Meudon, and chatted there some time with Madame de Saint-Simon on arriving. On account of the season we had little company. I left Madame de Saint-Simon in her cabinet, and went into mine.

About an hour after, at most, I heard cries and a sudden uproar. I ran out and I found Madame de Saint-Simon quite terrified, bringing to me a groom of the Marquis de Ruffec, who wrote to me from Versailles, that M. le Duc d'Orleans was in a apoplectic fit. I was deeply moved, but not surprised; I had expected it, as I have shown, for a long time. I impatiently waited for my carriage, which was a long while coming, on account of the distance of the new chateau from the stables. I flung myself inside; and was driven as fast as possible.

At the park gate I met another courier from M. de Ruffec, who stopped me, and said it was all over. I remained there more than half an hour absorbed in grief and reflection. At the end I resolved to go to Versailles, and shut myself up in my rooms; I learnt there the particulars of the event.

M. le Duc d'Orleans had everything prepared to go and work with the King. While waiting the hour, he chatted with Madame

Falari, one of his mistresses. They were close to each other, both seated in armchairs, when suddenly he fell against her, and never from that moment had the slightest glimmer of consciousness.

La Falari, frightened as much as may be imagined, cried with all her might for help, and redoubled her cries. Seeing that nobody replied, she supported as best she could this poor prince upon the contiguous arms of the two chairs, ran into the grand cabinet, into the chamber, into the ante-chambers, without finding a soul; finally, into the court and the lower gallery. It was the hour at which M. le Duc d'Orleans worked with the King, an hour when people were sure no one would come and see him, and that he had no need of them, because he ascended to the King's room by the little staircase from his vault, that is to say his wardrobe. At last La Falari found somebody, and sent the first who came to hand for help. Chance; or rather providence, had arranged this sad event at a time when everybody was ordinarily away upon business or visits, so that a full half-hour elapsed before doctor or surgeon appeared, and about as long before any domestics of M. le Duc d'Orleans could be found.

As soon as the faculty had examined the Regent; they judged his case hopeless. He was hastily extended upon the floor, and bled, but he gave not the slightest sign of life, do what they might to him. In an instant, after the first announcement, everybody flocked to the spot; the great and the little cabinet were full of people. In less than two hours all was over, and little by little the solitude became as great as the crowd had been. As soon as assistance came, La Falari flew away and gained Paris as quickly as possible.

La Vrilliere was one of the first who learnt of the attack of apoplexy. He instantly ran and informed the King and the Bishop of Frejus. Then M. le Duc, like a skilful courtier, resolved to make the best of his time; he at once ran home and drew up at all hazards the patent appointing M. le Duc prime minister, thinking it probable that that prince would be named. Nor was he deceived. At the first intelligence of apoplexy, Frejus proposed M. le Duc to the King, having probably made his arrangements in advance. M. le Duc arrived soon after, and entered the cabinet where he saw the King, looking very sad, his eyes red and tearful.

Scarcely had he entered than Frejus said aloud to the King, that in the loss he had sustained by the death of M. le Duc d'Orleans (whom he very briefly eulogised), his Majesty could not do better than beg M. le Duc, there present, to charge himself with everything, and accept the post of prime minister M. le Duc d'Orleans had filled. The King, without saying a word, looked at Frejus, and consented by a sign of the head, and M. le Duc uttered his thanks.

La Vrilliere, transported with joy at the prompt policy he had followed, had in his pocket the form of an oath taken by the prime minister, copied from that taken by M. le Duc d'Orleans, and proposed to Frejus to administer it immediately. Frejus proposed it to the King as a fitting thing, and M. le Duc instantly took it. Shortly after, M. le Duc went away; the crowd in the adjoining rooms augmented his suite, and in a moment nothing was talked of but M. le Duc.

M. le Duc de Chartres (the Regent's son), very awkward, but a libertine, was at Paris with an opera dancer he kept. He received the courier which brought him the news of the apoplexy, and on the road (to Versailles), another with the news of death. Upon descending from his coach, he found no crowd, but simply the Duc de Noailles, and De Guiche, who very 'apertement' offered him their services, and all they could do for him. He received them as though they were begging-messengers whom he was in a hurry to get rid of, bolted upstairs to his mother, to whom he said he had just met two men who wished to bamboozle him, but that he had not been such a fool as to let them. This remarkable evidence of intelligence, judgment, and policy, promised at once all that this prince has since performed. It was with much trouble he was made to comprehend that he had acted with gross stupidity; he continued, nevertheless, to act as before.

He was not less of a cub in the interview I shortly afterwards had with him. Feeling it my duty to pay a visit of condolence to Madame la Duchesse d'Orleans, although I had not been on terms of intimacy with her for a long while, I sent a message to her to learn whether my presence would be agreeable. I was told that Madame la Duchesse d'Orleans would be very glad to see me. I accordingly immediately went to her.

I found her in bed, with a few ladies and her chief officers around, and M. le Duc de Chartres making decorum do double duty for grief. As soon as I approached her she spoke to me of the grievous misfortune—not a word of our private differences. I had stipulated thus. M. le Duc de Chartres went away to his own rooms. Our dragging conversation I put an end to as soon as possible.

From Madame la Duchesse d'Orleans I went to M. le Duc de Chartres. He occupied the room his father had used before being Regent. They told me he was engaged. I went again three times during the same morning. At the last his valet de chambre was ashamed, and apprised him of my visit, in despite of me. He came across the threshold of the door of his cabinet, where he had been occupied with some very common people; they were just the sort of people suited to him.

I saw a man before me stupefied and dumfounded, not afflicted, but so embarrassed that he knew not where he was. I paid him the strongest, the clearest, the most energetic of compliments, in a loud voice. He took me, apparently, for some repetition of the Ducs de Guiche and de Noailles, and did not do me the honour to reply one word.

I waited some moments, and seeing that nothing would come out of the mouth of this image, I made my reverence and withdrew, he advancing not one step to conduct me, as he ought to have done, all along his apartment, but reburying himself in his cabinet. It is true that in retiring I cast my eyes upon the company, right and left, who appeared to me much surprised. I went home very weary of dancing attendance at the chateau.

The death of M. le Duc d'Orleans made a great sensation abroad and at home; but foreign countries rendered him incomparably more justice, and regretted him much more, than the French. Although foreigners knew his feebleness, and although the English had strangely abused it, their experience had not the less persuaded them of the range of his mind, of the greatness of his genius and of his views, of his singular penetration, of the sagacity and address of his policy, of the fertility of his expedients and of his resources, of the dexterity of his conduct under all changes of circumstances and events, of his clearness in considering objects and combining things;

of his superiority over his ministers, and over those that various powers sent to him; of the exquisite discernment he displayed in investigating affairs; of his learned ability in immediately replying to everything when he wished. The majority of our Court did not regret him, however. The life he had led displeased the Church people; but more still, the treatment they had received from his hands.

The day after death, the corpse of M. le Duc d'Orleans was taken from Versailles to Saint-Cloud, and the next day the ceremonies commenced. His heart was carried from Saint-Cloud to the Val de Grace by the Archbishop of Rouen, chief almoner of the defunct Prince. The burial took place at Saint-Denis, the funeral procession passing through Paris, with the greatest pomp. The obsequies were delayed until the 12th of February. M. le Duc de Chartres became Duc d'Orleans.

After this event, I carried out a determination I had long resolved on. I appeared before the new masters of the realm as seldom as possible— only, in fact, upon such occasions where it would have been inconsistent with my position to stop away. My situation at the Court had totally changed. The loss of the dear Prince, the Duc de Bourgogne, was the first blow I had received. The loss of the Regent was the second. But what a wide gulf separated these two men!